Engaged, Connected, Empowered

This reader-friendly book offers practical strategies and digital resources that will help K–12 students succeed in the 21st century. You will learn how to teach students to collaborate and make connections, filter primary source information, create products to demonstrate learning, develop a digital toolkit, and more!

Special Features:
- Digital resources are included to help you implement the ideas in this book.
- Personal anecdotes are provided from the authors' own successes and failures using technology.
- The book is organized by topic, so you can skip around and read or reread the parts that are relevant to you.
- The authors provide suggestions for teachers at different comfort levels with technology—novice, intermediate, and expert.
- The book's accompanying Facebook page includes additional content and links to complement the book (http://facebook.com/EngagedConnectedEmpowered).

Ben Curran is a co-founder of Engaging Educators, a company that helps teachers engage students in meaningful learning experiences. He is a former classroom teacher and current instructional coach.

Neil Wetherbee is a co-founder of Engaging Educators and a current elementary school classroom teacher.

Engaged, Connected, Empowered

Teaching and Learning in the 21st Century

Ben Curran and Neil Wetherbee

Routledge
Taylor & Francis Group

NEW YORK AND LONDON

First published 2014
by Routledge
711 Third Avenue, New York, NY 10017

and by Routledge
2 Park Square, Milton Park, Abingdon, Oxon OX14 4RN

Routledge is an imprint of the Taylor & Francis Group, an informa business

Notices
No responsibility is assumed by the publisher for any injury and/or damage to
persons or property as a matter of products liability, negligence or otherwise, or
from any use of operation of any methods, products, instructions, or ideas
contained in the material herein.

Practitioners and researchers must always rely on their own experience and
knowledge in evaluating and using any information, methods, compounds, or
experiments described herein. In using such information or methods they
should be mindful of their own safety and the safety of others, including
parties for whom they have a professional responsibility.

Product or corporate names may be trademarks or registered trademarks,
and are used only for identification and explanation without intent to infringe.

Library of Congress Cataloging-in-Publication Data
Curran, Ben.
  Engaged, connected, empowered : teaching and learning in the 21st century /
  Ben Curran and Neil Wetherbee.
      pages cm
  1. Creative teaching.   2. Student-centered learning.   3. Educational innovations.
  4. Education and globalization.   5. Educational change.
  I. Wetherbee, Neil.   II. Title.
  LB1025.3.C877 2013
  371.102—dc23   2013018245

ISBN: 978-0-415-73400-4 (hbk)
ISBN: 978-1-59667-255-0 (pbk)
ISBN: 978-1-315-85232-4 (ebk)

Typeset in Optima
by RefineCatch Limited, Bungay, Suffolk

Printed and bound in the United States of America by Publishers Graphics,
LLC on sustainably sourced paper.

Dedication

To our children who inspire and motivate us every day:
Annabel, Bennett, and Leo
and
Desi, Ada, and Hazel

Contents

Meet the Authors

Ben Curran was born and raised in Pontiac, Michigan. He earned his teaching degree from Eastern Michigan University and began his teaching career in 2000. Since then, he has taught, at various times, grades four through eight. He is currently employed as an instructional coach at a K–5 charter school in Detroit, Michigan.

In addition, he has taught educational technology workshops for his district and presented at several conferences, including those of the Michigan Association of Public School Academies, the Michigan Elementary and Middle School Principals Association, the Independent Schools Association of the Central States, and the International Society for Technology in Education.

In 2011, he co-founded Engaging Educators, a company dedicated to helping educators and families transform their learning environments in meaningful and exciting ways. Ben blogs actively for Engaging Educators at www.engagingeducators.com/blog and has written guest posts for the Teaching Channel and Education Week Teacher on various topics including poetry, educational technology, and the Common Core State Standards.

Ben lives outside Detroit and is the father of a daughter and two sons.

Neil Wetherbee grew up in Northport, Michigan. The public school district he attended was a member of the Coalition of Essential Schools. His relationship with the educational process was significantly shaped by the high expectations, personalization, and performance-based assessments found in these schools. He earned his teaching degree from the University of Michigan and has been teaching in Detroit at a school that encourages him to teach the way he believes since 2005.

More and more of Neil's teaching included the use of technology, so he sought formal training in the field of educational technology. He earned an Educational Technology Certificate and an M.A. in Educational Technology from Michigan State University. He regularly implements Web 2.0 technologies with an emphasis on course management systems to increase student engagement and achievement.

In addition to providing the educational technology professional development for the secondary teachers in his district, Neil has co-presented at many of the conferences with Ben.

Neil lives in Rochester, Michigan, with his wife and three daughters.

Acknowledgements

The authors have several people they'd like to thank. Without them, this book would not have been possible.

To Vicki Davis . . . for believing in us, giving us a shot, and sharing the stage not only to help get our name out there, but to help us achieve the dream of getting a book published.

To Barb Blackburn . . . for being one of the most helpful and friendly authors we know.

To Nan Gill . . . the principal who hired us both and gave us the freedom to teach in the manner we believe is best for kids.

To our PLN [personal learning network], the people we learn from every day . . . there are too many of you to list, but we need to specifically thank those friends whose work and stories helped improve this book: Steve Goldberg, Chris Henke-Mueller, and Ben Rimes.

To our editors, Lauren Beebe and Lauren Davis . . . you helped two novices feel like they belonged in the author business.

To Bob Sickles . . . for giving us a chance.

To our families . . . for their support and faith in us.

Ben would also like to thank . . .

Neil Wetherbee for putting up with his crazy ideas and being everything anyone could want in a co-author.

Braden Welborn of the Center for Teaching Quality for taking the time to help him become a better writer.

Jessy Irwin and Marialice Curran . . . two friends who encourage him and cheer him on.

The teachers who made a difference in his life . . . Mrs. O'Shaughnessy, Mrs. Green, Mrs. Wagner, Mr. Roller, and Mr. Richardson.

Neil would like to thank . . .

Ben Curran for introducing him to educational technology and making him write this book.

The high school teachers who helped him become the educator he is today . . . Mr. Steve Wetherbee, Mr. Dan Stowe, Mr. Phil Heller, Ms. Nancy Schaner, and Mrs. Donna Stowe.

To Deb Wetherbee . . . for spending countless hours being our first sanity check as we wrote this book.

Introduction

Our grandparents are in their 80s and 90s. Take a moment to ponder the vast changes that people our grandparents' ages have witnessed in their lifetimes. In about a century, they've seen the advent of television, space exploration, computers, fast food, air travel, phones that fit into people's pockets, surgery conducted with lasers, and cars that run on rechargeable batteries. The number of things that exist now that didn't exist when our grandparents were born has to number in the thousands. Nearly every aspect of life has undergone revolutionary change—except one: education.

One hundred years ago, school was somewhere students went every day from September to June. While they were there, a teacher stood in front of the class and told them what to do. Students sat. They listened. They learned. That's how school worked, and that's how it continues to work now. Walk into nearly any school in the United States and you are likely to find teachers standing in front of groups of students, telling them what to do and how to do it. Students are still expected to sit, listen, and learn. They fill in blanks on maps and worksheets, answer math problems they don't necessarily understand, recall dates and names, and perform a multitude of other tasks that do not require them to think critically, work together, analyze, evaluate, or problem solve.

Granted, today's classrooms have computers, interactive whiteboards, and a myriad of other gadgets and gizmos designed to "enhance" the learning experience. That certainly represents a change but only a change in the *stuff* used to teach children. Whether it's changing from blackboards to whiteboards or from overhead projectors to document cameras, teachers have added plenty of tools. There has not been, however, any sort of change in the *way* they teach, and while many educators strive to improve the quality of teaching and learning, the kinds of systemic reforms that we believe are needed are rarely discussed by the politicians and administrators who have the power to bring about these changes.

Why, though, is change needed? It's pretty simple. Schools are preparing students for a century that no longer exists. This is without a doubt a disservice to children, who are graduating unprepared to compete and participate in a global workplace.

How can it be that life has been altered in nearly every way except the way school works? The way people drive, travel, communicate, shop, eat, and so much more has changed. Why not the way teachers teach? In a world so different from the one that used to exist, a world that demands its citizens and workforce to innovate, create, collaborate, and communicate in entirely new ways, why are children still forced to learn in the same way? Why are educators overtesting them, loading them down with homework that requires rote memorization, and keeping them seated at desks all day? Why are teachers still using an educational model that is centuries old?

More importantly, though, what can be done? Educators have spent far too much time waiting for change to be imposed upon them by the powers that be. They wait for politicians to magically see the light and enact sweeping reforms that would eliminate standardized testing, unfair teacher evaluation systems, and other platforms and programs that keep American education stuck in a century gone by. It's time to stop *waiting* for change to happen and start *making* change happen. Our job here is to help you—whether you're a teacher, a parent, an administrator, a professor, a prospective educator, or a concerned citizen—make change a reality in your own realm.

These changes have to begin with acceptance. Teachers have to accept that there are some things out of their control: laws, standardized testing, socioeconomic status of students, and so on. Accepting that teachers cannot control these things and recognizing that there are plenty of things they can control is critical. In this book, we'll focus on five aspects of learning that *can* be changed.

We've been teaching together in the same school in Detroit, Michigan, since 2005. Within our own classrooms, we've worked to shift the process of teaching and learning in a way that better reflects the age we live in. Our students collaborate with one another and students around the world. They work actively and independently to direct their own learning, filtering and evaluating information, thinking critically, and solving problems on a regular basis. They produce detailed evidence of their learning instead of consuming information that we provide them. In short, they are preparing to be thinkers and learners—21st-century citizens, not the passive consumers required by the past.

We'll outline five shifts—consumption versus production, localized versus global, searching versus filtering, standardized versus student centered, and isolated versus connected—in teaching style and learner behavior. These shifts have happened in our own classrooms, and we'll describe them in ways that can be easily imitated in classrooms that you influence. The outcomes and benefits can be substantial: students who are prepared to live and work in the 21st century, students who are engaged every day, and students who are lifelong learners dedicated to making a positive impact on the world. Although this book is designed to be read from front to back, we have tried to make each shift, or section, independent of the rest; so you may notice ideas, such as hashtags, being defined in several different shifts. Furthermore, although we have worked mostly in upper elementary classrooms, the anecdotes and ideas we will share can be transferred and implemented in classrooms of all grades. However, be advised, this is *not* a book about technology. Yes, we do use technology in our classroom almost every day, and yes, technology is certainly beneficial, but *Engaged, Connected, Empowered: Teaching and Learning in the 21st Century* is about change: changing teaching, changing learning, and changing the world of education—one classroom at a time.

Interact with the authors and find ongoing content for this book at https://www.facebook.com/EngagedConnectedEmpowered.

Shift 1: Consumption Versus Production

1 An Introduction

In the traditional 20th-century classroom students consumed, or at least teachers hoped they consumed, the information presented to them. This style of teaching has been parodied numerous times on television and in movies. Just think of the boring teacher droning on and on in a monotone voice. The camera pans to the students, and none of them are engaged. Students are doodling and daydreaming. Unfortunately, the teacher thinks he's prepared a wonderful lesson on a topic that he, and everyone else, will think is enthralling. The sad thing is this parody plays out in classrooms across the United States every day because many teachers and schools are using an outdated 20th-century model. In this section, we'll examine one of the shifts from this outdated 20th-century model to a more engaging and effective 21st-century model.

We'll begin this shift by examining these areas:

- Students as "consumers" of information presented by their teachers
- Lack of challenge for students who are consumers
- Encouragement of students to produce evidence of their learning

Then, in the second and third parts of Shift 1, we will do the following:

- Show you a few simple steps to move from student consumption to student production
- Provide you with examples to further clarify

Consumers of Information

In a teacher-centered classroom, which is typical of the 20th-century model, the teacher does most of the hard work. The teacher has to find the resources that help teach the desired standards, then use those resources to create a presentation. Next, the teacher creates some sort of assessment to be sure that students have consumed the information presented and, finally, gives the presentation and assessment. In this scenario, the teacher is the producer and the student is the consumer. Additionally, the teacher is doing most of the work and perhaps the learning too.

Students should be doing most of the producing and, in turn, learning in a modern classroom. Student production is more challenging for students than mere consumption. Furthermore, production encourages students to develop thinking skills, particularly critical thinking skills. Although the teacher is still in charge of selecting standards, the students are responsible for finding or, at a minimum, using the resources. The students are responsible for synthesizing the information and creating the product.

In addition to the students learning, they are producing evidence of their learning. A product can use nondigital tools (markers, paper, etc.) or more modern technologies. Both kinds of products have advantages. The primary advantage of more traditional tools is that a limited access to computers, digital cameras, etc., is not a problem. Imagine your class is learning about World War II. Rather than preparing a lesson on D-day, challenge your students to create a product demonstrating what D-day was. Students could research and write poems about the events, create annotated maps, or produce diary entries from the perspective of a French citizen. In all these examples, the students are doing the research, synthesizing what they learned, and producing something. These products are tangible evidence of their learning. The same lesson could be addressed using more modern technologies, which tend to be flashy and more in keeping with the students of today. In this case, students could research D-day and write a script and record a podcast, create an annotated Google map that includes links and videos, or produce a VoiceThread around images of French citizens. These digital technologies aren't actually any better or worse than traditional tools, but the 21st-century method of presenting the topic is better.

We are in no way trying to devalue the importance of traditional assessments such as tests, but a well-designed project that includes student production provides much greater clarity of strengths and weaknesses because faking, cheating, or copying a final product is difficult. Cramming for a project is also difficult. These products demonstrate student learning. Furthermore, the products allow for diverse learning styles to succeed. Standard assessments suit the strengths of only a select group of students. Creating products allows for students of all intelligences to demonstrate their knowledge and growth and—most important—is fun and engaging.

Governor Richard Snyder of Michigan succinctly summarized the necessary change in educational methods in a special message on education reform on April 27, 2011. Although we don't agree with everything he wrote in that report, this quote captures the change from the 20th-century model to the 21st.

> But to compete on a world-wide scale, our education system must evolve from one that served us well in the past to one that embraces the challenges and opportunities of the new century. A grammar school education once suited the agrarian age, and a high-school education suited the assembly line age. A high-quality post-secondary education is needed for the technology age.
>
> (Snyder, 2011)

In the 19th century, a solid education prepared children to work on and run a farm. The 20th-century model prepared children to work on an assembly line. And clearly, especially in Governor Snyder's state of Michigan, assembly line jobs are becoming a career of the past. The number of manufacturing jobs available and the compensation for them has been falling steadily. Working on an assembly line is no longer a ticket to a stable, middle-class life. Therefore, we should not prepare our children for that career. We need to prepare children for the technology-age jobs that have already been created and help create flexible children who can adapt to fill the jobs not yet created. The 21st-century model focuses on creativity, collaboration, and knowledge acquisition through production, not consumption.

Perhaps you are left saying to yourself, "This all makes sense, but where do I go from here?" In Chapter 2, we will provide you with the tools necessary to get students producing. Chapter 3 will provide a summary of products we've used in our own classrooms. After reading all of Shift 1, "Consumption Versus Production," you will be inspired to implement many of these techniques, and you'll have the tools necessary to do so successfully.

2 Implementation

Educators use numerous excuses to convince themselves that they should resist change. Change can certainly seem scary, and some of the excuses are, on their surface, legitimate:

- My administration wants me to teach in a certain way.
- I don't have a curriculum that allows for production.
- It seems like a lot of work for the teacher.
- How do I really know students are learning?
- I don't have enough time.

These, however, are merely excuses. It's all right to feel apprehensive to change, but sometimes change is necessary. In the case of education in the 21st century, this is certainly the case. The jump from student consumption to production may seem overwhelming at first. It's all about baby steps, however. In the end, after gradual implementation, you will understand the power of student production. In this chapter, we will explain the importance and the how of moving from student consumption to student production through the following key elements:

- Creating engaging learning experiences in which students become producers
- Developing a digital tool kit to produce evidence of students' learning
- Assessing products using rubrics
- Using social bookmarking and reflective digital portfolios as students shift to becoming curators of knowledge

Engagement

It would be difficult, if not impossible, for someone to successfully argue that more learning occurs when students are passive than active. No teacher has ever asked for passive listening or passive participation. Active listening and active participation are two keys to successful learning anytime in life. With this being said, sage-on-the-stage, direct instruction, is rarely active. By its very definition, the heavy lifting in direct instruction is done by the teacher. It is hard to be active when someone else is doing much of the work.

In his book *Drive: The Surprising Truth About What Motivates Us*, Daniel Pink very effectively explains the three elements of motivation: autonomy, mastery, and purpose. In his cocktail summary, he explains: "Autonomy—the desire to direct our own lives. Mastery—the urge to get better and better at something that matters. Purpose—the yearning to do what we do in the service of something larger than ourselves" (Daniel H. Pink). Although he is writing about motivation, motivation goes hand in hand with engagement. It is difficult to get even one of these elements of motivation in a direct instruction lesson in which students are merely consuming information, and it's nearly impossible to get two or more. However, a well-designed project that involves student production easily hits all three elements.

When students are given an opportunity to produce evidence of their learning, they are given some autonomy. There is no one way to get to a right answer. Students are able to direct their learning based on their individual needs, interests, and skills.

For many students, the consumption of information matters only to do well on a test or get a good grade. Most people don't set a life goal of doing well on worksheets derived from textbooks. However, most, if not all, take pride in producing something of high quality. Students eagerly revise products to make them the best they can be. Presenting to an authentic audience, such as local experts or people on the Internet, students are increasingly motivated to work toward mastery.

Purpose is the hardest of the three elements to find through student production. However, looking at the converse makes it much more evident. Simply consuming information in no way feeds the yearning to do something that's larger than ourselves. Activities that involve student production can be framed in a greater purpose. Students can create a wiki about a book for other students to use and learn from. Students can create videos of their poetry to put on YouTube for others to watch and enjoy. More examples can be found in Chapter 3 of this book. Finding purpose for student productions is key to obtaining full motivation and engagement.

Step 1: A Tool Kit

What Is a Tool Kit?

The first step in moving toward student production is developing a digital tool kit. In our teaching, we use the terms *tool kit, toolbox,* and *tool belt* interchangeably when teaching children and adults. These phrases represent a set of skills that can be used. For example, after teaching a lesson on metaphors, we might ask students to add metaphors to their tool belts. Or later on, we might ask students to use something from their toolboxes, such as metaphors, to make their writing more engaging. Teachers and students need a digital tool kit so they can produce evidence of their learning.

These tool belts are built gradually and intentionally. Start with one tool, and grow from there. The amazing thing with most children, though, is that many of them need little or no help learning to use a new tool. They just need a point in the right direction. In the beginning of the school year, we try to introduce a variety of tools. The tools generally fall into three categories: audio, visual, and text based.

We have tools that we are quite partial to, but the speed at which the tools come and go makes it difficult for us to make recommendations. Even while writing this book, our favorite Web-based podcasting site decided to go in a "new company direction." There are, however, some tools that have withstood the test of time and look as if they should be around for a while. For Mac users, there are iMovie and GarageBand, and for PCs, there are Audacity and Windows Movie Maker. The Linux platform offers Audacity and OpenShot Video Editor. The tools available are bound to grow and change, so the best place to look for tools to add to your tool kit is your personal learning network (PLN), the people from whom you learn, as discussed in Shift 5 of this book, "Isolated Versus Connected."

What Do I Do with This Tool Kit?

We nearly always suggest starting with the end in mind, but we won't harp on that until Step 2 of this chapter. To begin with, pick an activity you already do in your class—perhaps something timeless and somewhat boring, such as a book report. There is a chance that the book reports your students are doing are nearly identical to the reports you did as a student. Pick a tool, such as a wiki (more to come on wikis later in this chapter), and have students create their book reports using a wiki rather than by hand or a word processor. This will allow for the use of multimedia and a larger, authentic audience. Obviously, book reports don't apply to all subjects or all teaching styles, but the logic holds true regardless of subject or content. These kinds of shifts are only a small adjustment to traditional 20th-century teaching methods. As you become more comfortable, increase the frequency and size of the shift.

Step 2: Assessment

Start with the End in Mind

Now that you've begun to develop your digital tool kit and your students have had a few experiences with production, start with the end in mind. Think of the standards and objectives you want students to master from this project, and work backward from there—perhaps something students have had a hard time grasping in the past. An example could be adding and subtracting fractions with unlike denominators. Begin the lesson with your regular direct instruction, but let students know that they are going to have to produce evidence of their learning at the end of this small project. Depending on your comfort level, you can go as far as saying, "Pick a tool from your tool kit, and demonstrate how to add and subtract fractions with unlike denominators." Provide students with a rubric of what is expected of them (more to come about rubrics in this step). Allow students to choose how they want to explain adding and subtracting fractions. Some students might choose something simple, such as PowerPoint, and others might choose to create a movie or talking animated cartoon. Regardless, at the end, students will have produced evidence of their learning, or their lack of learning will be apparent. This is not to say you shouldn't use traditional assessments too, but these productions will elicit more effort and produce better information for you.

Assess Student Productions

Traditional assessments, particularly multiple choice questions (sometimes called selected response), only provide evidence of correct or incorrect answers. Unless several questions assess the same objective, ruling out guessing is difficult. Even short-answer questions are generally graded correct or incorrect. Unfortunately, almost nothing in life is truly black and white.

Assessments, whether formative or summative, should accurately assess what students understand and which areas need more work. The most powerful currency of today might be data. Why else would a website such as Facebook be worth $100 billion at its initial IPO, even though it is a free service. It's all about the value of data. When teachers assess students, they should collect data that can be used to increase understanding and effective teaching. I want to know if Tommy got a question wrong because he didn't understand the concept of long division or because he simply thought for a moment that $6 \times 5 = 35$. Teachers need this data.

When students produce evidence of their learning, it is easy to assess correctness and understanding. A rubric is the simplest way to accomplish this. It is paramount that rubrics assess the objectives and standards being assessed, and they should be designed prior to beginning the project. That may seem obvious and perhaps redundant, but it is very important and not always done correctly. For example, if a student is creating an illustration to explain how the tilt of the Earth's axis causes the seasons, the rubric should focus more heavily, if not entirely, on the science and not the artistic ability.

Quite often, creating a teacher version and a student version of the rubric is beneficial. The teacher version can be much more precise and tied to standards and objectives. The student version can be the exact same rubric written in student-friendly terms. As an example, the teacher rubric might come directly from Common Core State Standard W.5.1b: "Provide logically ordered reasons that are supported by facts and details" (National Governors Association Center for Best Practices, Council of Chief State School Officers, 2010). This would mean very little to fifth-grade students. Their rubric might say "My reason makes sense and has evidence to help explain it because ___." The student rubric should be given to students at the beginning of an activity or project so they know exactly how they are going to be assessed. Furthermore, there is no question more infuriating to a teacher than, "Is this good enough?" Providing students with a student-friendly rubric allows them to self-check their work. The simple answer then is, "Have you checked the rubric?" Typically, this answer is sufficient, but there are always those children who want further hand-holding or who don't accurately assess their own work. Simply having students explain their reasons for giving themselves scores allows you to better see their thinking and helps you direct them to meet the objectives laid out in the rubric.

Rubrics are fantastic guides for students to use in their developing learning, and they are wonderful formative and summative assessments.

Step 3: Curators' Knowledge

The quantity of information in the world only continues to grow. In order for information to be meaningful, it needs to be organized. Students can easily organize others' information and evidence of their own learning. The process of organizing information further increases understanding and produces additional evidence of learning.

Others' Knowledge

Although this chapter is about student production, rather than consumption, of knowledge, there is benefit in organizing the knowledge of others. The amount of information available today is overwhelming, and we will go into methods of filtering useful information in Shift 3 of this book, "Searching Versus Filtering"; however, the collection of information can serve as a valuable method of student production.

Students need to organize the work of others not only for their own use but also for others'. Social bookmarking is one example of this. With social bookmarking, people's bookmarks are made visible for all people to use, unless marked as private. Social bookmarks are organized through tagging, which makes them easy to sort and filter. Students should conduct research, read articles, work on projects, etc., and should catalog and tag useful sites. This collection of knowledge will follow them wherever they go, even beyond your classroom or their graduation. Furthermore, these bookmarks can be used by others, which is always motivating.

Although there are student-friendly bookmarking sites, it is possible to create collections of others' work through the creation of websites, such as wikis. Students can gather resources and links around different topics. For example, *The Wednesday Wars*, by Gary D. Schmidt, is set in the late 1960s and contains numerous references to an era that may be confusing to students of today. Students can research these references, such as Bing Crosby and the Vietnam War. Additionally, the book contains references to topics that may not be understood by all members of society. Many of our students were unfamiliar with lima beans and cream puffs. Students can research these topics and create wikis explaining what these references mean. This activity of synthesizing the work of others benefits students through an increased understanding of the text, and it provides them with an opportunity to create something meaningful to themselves and others.

Own Knowledge

As students produce more and more evidence of their own learning, they need some way to catalog, display, and organize their productions. There is no better way to do this than through the creation of digital portfolios. Digital portfolios are more than just warehouses of student work; they are repositories of knowledge and learning.

Digital portfolios allow for continuing growth. There is no reason that a child's portfolio couldn't start in kindergarten and run through 12th grade. This might require some district planning and vertical alignment, but it shouldn't be much work. If students are allowed to use their full names, they can begin to create positive digital footprints, which is critical these days. It is of the utmost importance that a Google search of one's name turns up positive information. Students have the ability to shape their footprints into what they want and need for future success through products such as digital portfolios.

Portfolios allow for student reflection. It is essential for all people, regardless of age, to reflect on their work. Digital portfolios allow students to write about their learning and what they have produced. In many cases the reflection is more important than the original product. Students need to reflect on what worked or didn't work and why, what they learned, how they would do it differently next time, whether their product matched the expectations on the rubric, etc. It is this reflection that causes growth and improvement from project to project. Without a portfolio, much of this reflecting does not happen or does not have a tangible purpose.

The level of complexity for digital portfolios is up to those creating them. In the lower grades, this choice is most likely made by the teacher. As students grow older, they may have more say about which tool they want to use to create their portfolios. Think back to the autonomy element mentioned earlier in the chapter. The ultimate choice of tool will come from which tools are in your digital tool kit. A safe place to start is a wiki. Wikis are simple to use, straightforward, and widely accepted throughout education. The next level, which means increased difficulty but higher-end finished products, is Google Sites (or whatever they change the name to next). Numerous other tools have the potential to go above and beyond these tools. Digital portfolios can also be made with blogs, with course management software, and through sites designed specifically for digital portfolios or e-portfolios. These last two options may cost money, and we try to promote only free tools. Regardless of how a digital portfolio is made, it is a key element of successful student production—especially when the element of reflection is used.

What Have We Learned?

- Student engagement increases with production.
- 21st-century citizens need a digital tool kit.
- Learning products are easily assessed through rubrics.
- Students learn from being curators of knowledge.

What Now?

You've decided that you need to shift from student consumption to student production. Here are some basic steps, depending on your current abilities.

NOVICE:
Start small. Find an activity or a project you have planned, and incorporate a simple learning product at the end. This totally goes against the key premise of starting with the end in mind, but the teaching gods will forgive you just this one time.

INTERMEDIATE:
Start with the end in mind. Find that key objective you really want your students to understand. Think about how students could demonstrate an understanding of this objective. Design an activity or a project that works toward an understanding of the objective. Be sure the activity or project has students producing some evidence of their learning.

EXPERT:

1. Have students start to warehouse their products in digital portfolios. Be sure that students reflect on their work.

2. Add elements of global collaboration with student production. Have students work with other students around the world to collaboratively produce evidence of their learning. More on this in Shift 2 of this book, "Localized Versus Global."

3   **Anecdotes**

Our own experiences have created many opportunities to shift our students from consumers of content and information to producers of learning artifacts. We've shown you how you can do this in Chapter 2. In this chapter, we will share our stories.

We aren't expecting you to execute each of these activities exactly as we did. Our hope is that you'll find enough inspiration within this chapter to make the shift yourselves. It's not so much about copying what we have done as it is about shifting your mind-set to empower students to create. Once you start looking at teaching through the prism of production, the sky's the limit. You'll find inspiration everywhere.

It is also not our intention to go through every step of every project. This would prove overwhelming and might distract from our core purpose. Instead, take these ideas and build off them, modify them, expand them, and make them your own. When it comes to student production of learning artifacts, the good news is that you don't have to reinvent the wheel. Soon, however, you'll find that you're coming up with your own ideas to engage students in your own way. You'll get to the point where all it takes is a photograph, a line from a story, a question on *Jeopardy*, or a newspaper story to get you thinking "What could my students make out of this?"

Just remember, one of the greatest benefits to student-produced work is that it can be shared with a global audience. Not only does this serve as a huge motivator for students and teachers alike, but it also can be very powerful for students to realize that the work they create may help others learn, not just now, but for years to come. Keep this in mind as you analyze these stories.

Life, Liberty, and the Pursuit of Video

One of our first projects together involved core democratic values (CDV), those key principles that make the American government and way of life unique and special. The only problem? These principles—among them diversity, the common good, and popular sovereignty—can be very difficult for elementary and middle school students to grasp. Comprehending them, however, is crucial for success in high school history and civics courses (and, where we live, mastering the state standardized tests).

We decided to present the values in a short series of mini-lessons, complete with examples and ample time for questions and discussion. But then we put things in the hands of the students, asking them to create digital videos that demonstrate an understanding of the CDV. We set forth two challenges: find digital images that represent the value selected and include in the video an explanation of what the value means and its importance to our country.

This approach proved successful for many reasons. Students were empowered to create the videos however they saw fit. We did provide them with an opportunity to storyboard their videos by sketching and writing scripts. (We do this with nearly every audio or video project, automatically embedding writing into the experience in an authentic way.)

This project was also successful because it took some very abstract concepts and challenged students to express them in concrete ways, with both images and speech. Each child was very successful, making it clear that they understood the values and their importance to our society. It was exciting to see.

Take a Look; It's in a Book

As with all projects we embark on, we began with the end in mind. As a part of our balanced literacy curriculum, our students are supposed to write book recommendations and conduct book talks. A book talk is basically a few-minute tease that tries to entice others to read the book. After five years of trying to have our students complete successful book recommendations and talks, we were becoming quite frustrated with the poor quality and overall lack of success.

We took a step back and reflected on successful book talks we'd seen in the past. As children of the 80s, we thought back to a television show that made even the worst books look exciting. We went to our local library and checked out *Reading Rainbow* DVDs. As a class, we watched the book reviews that were always a part of *Reading Rainbow*.

Using the videos as motivation and a model, students picked picture books from the class library and wrote book-talk scripts for their books. Students then worked together to film them reciting their scripts in front of a green screen. Because our school uses Macs, we used the advanced features on iMovie to turn the green screen into a superimposed image of their books. Most modern video-editing software now contains this feature.

Students were totally engaged and motivated by this product. The end result was a wonderful class set of well-written book talks. Our classes then projected their videos for our school's literacy night. Everyone was impressed, and it was nice to have our students displaying something higher order on Bloom's Taxonomy.

Alternative Math Assessments

Toward the end of a school year, we wanted to conduct a summative assessment. We began by having our students brainstorm a list of all the math concepts they had learned throughout the year. The list neared 40 items. We then had them brainstorm a list of tools they've learned to demonstrate learning. The list included tools such as PowerPoint, podcasts, videos, cartoons using Xtranormal, and about twenty other tools. We then had a lottery in which each student selected a math concept and a tool to demonstrate his or her learning. To create a more authentic experience, we promised to post all well-made and accurate projects on our class blogs for future students to reference and use. The final products turned out from average to good, but two special side effects occurred as a result of this project.

A student with a diagnosed learning disability really wanted to produce a product of some kind. He decided to produce a talking cartoon teaching how to add and subtract fractions with unlike denominators. When he began producing his cartoon, he had no understanding of adding and subtracting fractions with unlike denominators, but he was determined to produce something. He turned to his classmates and friends to teach him how to do the math. They did, and he learned. Because the cartoon characters read phonetically, he also was forced to improve his spelling and punctuation to have the characters read what he wanted them to say.

The other extremely positive outcome from creating these products came from a girl in one of our classes. She regularly refused to double-check her work or revise and edit her writing; she didn't like putting forth any effort beyond the minimum required. She decided to create a video for her project with one of our personal camcorders. She filmed her video in the hall outside our room. After class was over and the students were gone, we looked at that camcorder, and she had filmed no fewer than twenty takes of her video. When the learning is authentic, students want to work harder.

These student productions are still on our class blogs, and our new students still use them and are inspired to create their own.

4 Icons to Rule Them All

In a later chapter, we'll go into great detail about how important developing a personal learning network is. In the meantime, however, we offer up this example of the great ideas and inspiration that exist in the edublogosphere and within other social networks.

We learned of something called the 4 Icon Challenge from Ben Rimes, a fellow Michigander, educator, and blogger. His blog, TechSavvyEd.net, is amazing, and he shared the challenge in a post. The students' task is to find four digital images, or icons, that represent the essence of a story.

When we first read about this project, our classes were finishing a rich and complex novel called *A Wrinkle in Time*, by Madeleine L'Engle. One of the main learning objectives for our study of this book involved examining and recognizing universal themes. We thought the 4 Icon Challenge would be just right for this type of novel and for this particular objective. So we assigned the challenge and allowed students about three total hours to work on it. What we wanted to see was whether the students, without our steering them in that direction, would select images related to the book's many themes.

Did they ever! They used pictures of friends, family, and hearts to symbolize friendship, importance of family, and love—all critical *Wrinkle* themes—to create their iconic quartet. One student who felt identity and individualism were themes (we agree!) chose a picture of two kids dressed in punk rock attire. "They're being themselves," he explained, "just like Meg (the main character) needed to learn how to do."

This was an excellent assessment of the depth of students' under-standing of the novel and a great creative outlet. It also turned out to be a good way to practice speaking—the kids recorded their explanations using a site called VoiceThread. On top of all that, we also got to teach about the importance of copyright and fair use. Students were required to use only images that were licensed for reuse.

The 4 Icon Challenge is one that could be used for any book you read with students or even for an exploration of historical or current events. It's simple, easy, fun, and worthwhile, too.

A Note on Digital Images

We are sticklers for citing sources and being responsible digital citizens. Our students use a lot of digital images in their work, which leads to some meaningful discussions about copyright. It is important for students to respect the intellectual and creative property of others, instead of treating the Internet like one giant grab bag of content to be consumed and repurposed without consent.

When it comes to digital images, we teach our students that they aren't allowed to simply reuse any image on the Web they want to. This violation of copyright is unethical and against the law. We also teach them about Creative Commons, an organization that has created a set of copyright rules and licenses that are suited for the sharing nature of the Internet. There are many levels of Creative Commons licenses, with most granting permission for reuse—and some even allowing revision and remix.

We teach students how to search *only* for images that are licensed for reuse. (For sources of Creative Commons images, check out our Facebook page, http://facebook.com/EngagedConnectedEmpowered.) We also teach them how to cite the sources of the images they include in their work, just as a writer has to cite the texts he or she uses when researching a book or paper. So whether it's a video, blog post, slideshow, or PowerPoint, all images must be chosen responsibly, and credit must be given to the source.

I Believe in the Power of Love

We are avid National Public Radio (NPR) listeners. For several years in the early 2000s, NPR played *This I Believe* essays. Each essay focuses on a person's core belief, ranging from hilarious to extremely serious, from young to old, and from believable to unbelievable.

When unit planning for the year and looking through the state standards, we saw that writing an essay was a requirement. We immediately thought about *This I Believe.* We began our essay unit by streaming a couple of essays that had been played on the radio. We also printed the transcript of the essays. (These resources and more for educators can be found at thisibelieve.org/.) Students, with our help, analyzed these essays to see what made them successful. They also looked at the transcripts to see the parts of a standard essay. Most important, the essays inspired our students.

Students then wrote scripts (or what most of us would call essays) about what they believe in. After writing their essays, students used GarageBand and Aviary to record their own radio essay podcasts. The writing and subsequent recordings were truly inspiring. We couldn't believe what our students produced. Who would expect a fifth grader to eloquently write about their belief in the power of love? What they produced was infinitely more powerful and lasting than what would have resulted if they had read random essays or written essays about an imposed topic. This authentic activity helped us believe in the power of production.

Exploring Current Events

In one of the most satisfying projects of our careers, we led fifth graders in an exploration of events that were occurring in Syria in early 2012. At the time, the country was in a state of upheaval. Syrian citizens were protesting the rule of the nation's president, Bashar al-Assad. These protests were being violently shut down by the government and the Syrian army. Thousands were killed in the violence. It was a tense time, especially for many of the more than 40,000 Arab Americans living in Dearborn, Michigan, a city just five miles from our school.

With the help of fellow educator and Twitter friend Steve Goldberg, the classes undertook a month-long exploration of the country, centered on the idea that we could become "experts" in the complexities of this story. The end goal was to create a website that would educate other children around the world about what was going on in Syria. The content, however, would not be up to Steve or us: it would be completely up to the students. They chose what they thought people needed to know about the situation and the country.

After several class sessions of research, done by reading news articles and watching video, students then broke the content into several questions, which included these: Where is Syria? What is its basic history? Who lives there? Why are the people rebelling? Who is al-Assad? How does this uprising connect with the Arab Spring? What is the United Nations? Should the U.N. be involved in Syria?

Small groups each built one page of a wiki that answered its question in student-friendly language. They also created narrated screencasts of images related to the news stories we were reading, as well as video podcasts and a blog. These products now stand as both a testament to their learning and dedication and as a resource for others to use to learn about the topic.

Seeing young children accomplish and produce things that most wouldn't expect them to be able to can bring goose bumps. Watching students explore and create was rewarding and exciting. Knowing that what they were doing was intended to help educate the world about a tragic human rights crisis took it to another level of inspiration.

And this is certainly a type of exploration that could be replicated with any sort of news story—local, national, or international. Our students' work had depth. It involved reading, geography, history, writing, and even math (for example, "What percentage of the world's population is Muslim?").

This activity was also highly engaging. Students were so excited to learn about the news that they expanded their work to other stories, particularly stories of local interest. They became, perhaps, the only 10-year-old "experts" not only on the country of Syria but on the top news stories of their hometown as well.

Grammar Reenvisioned

The study of grammar causes many issues for educators: how to teach it, how often to teach it, how to make it interesting and engaging, how to teach it in a way that students will remember. We won't claim to have solved all these riddles, but we were able to approach the study of grammar and language in a unique way that led to the production of some terrific videos.

It started, as it often does, with inspiration from someone else's project. In this case we were inspired by the folks at Common Craft. They're the geniuses behind a series of videos that explains things in "plain English." Using nothing more than a white background and a few words and drawings (and a hand moving them around on the screen), Common Craft creates short videos that explain everything from the electoral college to wikis to zombie attack survival.

First, we showed students a couple of Common Craft examples. We love using models when we launch an activity so students have a clear idea of what to do. Ideally, we use samples of work from previous students of ours. When those aren't available, we locate others or make samples ourselves.

After this, we assigned groups of students a grammar rule or definition. Their task was to design videos in the Common Craft style that would teach kids about their grammar concepts.

One group made a video about the different types of nouns, one about how to use commas in a series, another about how and when to capitalize titles, one about when to properly use *there*, *their*, and *they're*, and so on.

Students planned, rehearsed, and shot their videos over the course of a few class periods and shared them with the world via the Web. And they shared them with each other—allowing them to learn these language rules from one another rather than from a lecture or a worksheet.

Bringing Words to Life

We're poetry nuts. We love reading it, teaching it, and teaching students how to write it. We also love trying to figure out ways to put a modern, digital twist on the study and writing of poems. Why? Because we figure if we can provide 21st-century students with a means of enjoying poems, we're more likely to hook them on the genre. Here's how we came up with a video project that challenged students to translate poems into digital images.

Poetry is all about imagery. A poem can conjure up beautiful and wondrous images in a reader's mind. And as writers of poetry, we want our students to be able to conjure those kinds of images, too. Luckily the Web's vast array of digital images and photographs can help in both regards.

Langston Hughes wrote two poems that we love to share with our students: "The Negro Speaks of Rivers" and "My People." They are rich in language and connotation. Simply put, they are powerful works of art. But there is much more to each of them than just the words on the page. Poems like these can be challenging for students to enjoy. Students can get lost in the complexities of a seemingly simple poem. Or sometimes the complexities are not even obvious to them. In the case of "The Negro Speaks of Rivers" and "My People" and other poems, Hughes has written pieces that are about much more than rivers and much more than faces and eyes. But how do we get students to visualize this? How do we help them to translate powerful words into images in their minds and to demonstrate that they grasp these poems' (or any poem's) complexities?

We decided to have students create videos that combined the text of the poem with digital images. Students searched photo sites for images that they connected with each poem; then they arranged these images using movie-editing software. (All images were licensed for reuse; see the sidebar "A Note on Digital Images.") They added the text of each poem to the movies, as well as some background music that fit the tone of the poem. These details offered beautiful visual representations of the poems. (This activity also works well with students writing their own poems and then finding images to match.)

In the end, our original objective—demonstrating an understanding of the poems' deeper meanings and rich imagery—was achieved. Students' videos were compelling and impressive. Seeing how different students interpreted the poems in vastly different ways was also interesting. We had them wrap up the assignment by watching one another's videos and writing about why they chose the pictures they did. Then we discussed how differently everyone pictured things in their minds when reading the same poem.

When we think of the things we want students to be able to do with a text—summarize, analyze, compare, etc.—it is only natural that we have them create something to demonstrate their understanding. The poetry videos are just one example of these types of creations. And in addition to being engaging and fairly quick to execute, this project incorporated all the essential language arts skills: writing, reading, speaking, and listening.

Video Did *Not* Kill the Radio Star

We have audio to thank for getting us into educational technology. Audio projects were among the first tech activities we ever taught our students how to create. Of course, we didn't call them something bland like "audio projects." We called them the cutting edge phrase—cue the trumpets—*podcasts.*

At the time (2007) podcasts were far from mainstream. Podcasts had only become available on the Apple Store only a few years prior (source: Wikipedia), and many in education, at least those with whom we ran, hadn't even heard of them yet. We were entering uncharted territory in more ways than one—we really didn't exactly know what we were doing. We essentially had to teach ourselves how to produce, record, and publish student podcasts. And then we had to figure out a method to incorporate them into the curriculum in meaningful ways.

We were incredibly excited by the challenge. The concept of putting student voices onto the Web for the world to hear really appealed to us. The idea that their recordings could potentially be heard by listeners on the other side of the globe was thrilling, and so was the thought that their podcasts might remain "live" on the Web for eternity, allowing their children and children's children to listen to their parents' and grandparents' learning from decades past.

The students got hooked on podcasting, just as we assumed they would. They loved working together to write scripts, rehearse, and record. They loved adding music, which we called "phat beats." They loved our "premiere parties," to which parents would be invited and we'd play everyone's podcast.

We loved it, too—not just because our students were having so much fun but also because they were using this new media to produce evidence of learning and understanding. Through these simple audio recordings, they showed us that they had learned what we were teaching. And as a bonus, they had a great time doing it. To this day, our students' podcasts, especially those early attempts, remain some of our favorite teaching memories. Whether it's the recording of a social studies game show, an audio diary of a historical figure, an interview with book characters, 60-second science reports, or any of the other great ideas they came up with, our students' podcasts turned out to be an engaging, useful, and easy means of assessing learning and challenging students to be creative and have fun.

The Engaging Educators' Podcast Tips

Follow these tips for an exciting and successful podcasting experience:

1. First, figure out what you want students to learn. What skills are you teaching? What do you want students to understand at the end of the project? It's about the learning, not the technology, so consider your desired outcomes first.

2. Always include writing. Every audio project we do requires a script. This not only pushes students to think carefully and plan but also weaves some writing into the experience.

3. Always require rehearsal. Students should record it as they say it. They need to work on getting rid of that "I'm reading it off my paper" tone of voice.

4. Kill the background noise. You'd be amazed what your computer's mic will pick up. Help students find a quiet place to record.

5. Advise students to break the work into several clips and record them one at a time. This has two advantages: If there's an error, students can rerecord the short segment easily. Also, with short clips, transition music can be inserted easily, making the podcast more interesting and professional sounding.

6. Encourage students to find some music for the introduction and conclusion—but nothing that violates copyrights. Even better: have kids create their own using GarageBand or another similar music-creation Web tool.

7. Upload the podcast to the Web. The recording does no good sitting on your hard drive. Using a podcasting service will automatically create a feed for folks to subscribe to. Also publishing your students' podcasts to iTunes boosts exposure—and kids get a kick out of being on iTunes.

8. Have students reflect, reflect, reflect. Their first try will not be their best. But it's important for students to reflect on each podcast they create. During this time, they can examine what went well—and not so well. Was it loud enough? Could you hear the shuffling of paper? Did someone talk in the middle of it? Careful reflection after a podcasting project has concluded can help students improve with each effort.

Words Matter, Too

It isn't always about video and audio for us. Our students have produced several blogging projects that showcase their writing to the world. One of the biggest motivators we've had for students when it comes to writing is through empowering them to write for a global audience via blogs. When students know that people from around the world are going to read what they write, they invariably pay closer attention to the finer details that are often skimmed over during traditional writing assignments, such as

Figure 3.1 Bracket for Student Writing

capitalization, grammar, and punctuation. They are invested deeply in their work, and as a result the quality of writing improves.

One of our students' favorite blogging projects involved persuasive writing. We started the project in March, right around the time of the NCAA basketball tournament. We told students we were holding a tournament of our own, a tournament of inventions, to determine the greatest invention of all time. Unlike the basketball tournament, however, a game would not determine the winner—a blog post would.

After we created a bracket (see Figure 3.1), students chose a pairing and selected a "team" to write in favor of. The writing was posted to a blog, and we invited blog readers to vote for the most persuasive piece. This included teachers in our school and other schools in our district, parents, other students, and readers around the world with the help of the Twitter hashtag #comments4kids. Those with the most votes advanced.

This started the way all good projects should, with a specific skill we wanted to teach: in this case, persuasive writing. Our challenge was trying to figure out an engaging way for students to produce persuasive writing for a worldwide audience.

Blogging is such an easy way to get students' work out into the world. It's a way for them to express themselves, write with an engaging voice, and practice using a popular modern tool.

It is multifunctional, as well. Blogging can be used in nearly every academic subject and beginning as young as first grade (or younger if you want to create an audio blog). Here are some ideas for class blogging projects.

Students could use a blog as a place to write the following:

- book reviews
- reflections on current events
- math learning logs
- poetry
- digital stories

What do all these examples have in common? The students are in charge. They do the heavy lifting—and the learning. Teachers worked hard to set up students for success—by providing the know-how, the tutorials, the time, and the inspiration to create—but then we backed out of the way. (You'll read more about how to make this "stepping back" a reality in Shift 4, "Standardized Versus Student Centered.")

There are so many ways for students to become producers of content. Keep production in mind as you plan projects and activities. Empower students by teaching them creation skills. Then allow them to produce evidence of learning using any tool they see fit. And keep in mind the key ideas of authenticity and audience. Producing authentic work for a wide-ranging audience is a critical element of a 21st-century classroom. Student work today can be broadcast to (and have an impact on) the world. And it should be.

Shift 2: Localized Versus Global

An Introduction

No matter how old you are, if you are reading this sentence, the following is certainly true: the world is a vastly different place than it was when you were in school. It is also true that the differences increase with each subsequent generation. In this section, we will explore one of the greatest shifts of the last generation and its influence on the world of education: the shift from a *local* focus to a *global* one.

In today's world, an educator can connect his or her school or classroom to locations around the world, engaging students in rich, meaningful educational experiences along the way. As Thomas Friedman (2007) so famously wrote, "the world is flat." Friedman explained:

> Clearly, it is now possible for people more than ever to collaborate and compete in real time with more other people on more different kinds of work from more different corners of the planet and on a more equal footing than at any previous time in the history of the world—using computers, e-mail, fiber-optic networks, teleconferencing and dynamic new software . . . we are now connecting all the knowledge centers on the planet into a single global network.
>
> (p. 8)

The impact of these words, of the reality of the 21st century and all that is possible, is just now beginning to be felt in our nation's classrooms. As educators Vicki Davis and Julie Lindsay (2012) reveal in their work, not only has the world been flattened but so have the walls of classrooms. In projects such as Davis and Lindsay's Flat Classroom projects, the possibilities that Friedman described are brought to life. So much is possible, but there is much more that can be done on a wider scale. In this section, we will look at some of these global "flattenings" and how they impact education.

We'll begin this shift by exploring these areas:

- Global has become the new local.
- The role of education in the global economy is changing.
- The need for global citizenship is increasing.

Then, in Chapters 5 and 6 of this section, we will do the following:

- Provide ways of connecting with other classrooms on your own and through existing projects
- Share our own stories and experiences with global collaborative projects

Global, the New Local

Let's dig into this idea of a flattened world more deeply. Whether you've realized it or not, the definition of the word *local* has shifted. No longer does the word simply refer to your own neighborhood, municipality, or region. Because you now have access to information and resources from all over the globe, you're as close to places thousands of miles away as you are to the corner store. Just as paved roads and automobiles revolutionized transportation at the turn of the 20th century, technology has revolutionized education in the 21st.

This shift is a critical one for educators to understand. They now have the ability to work with classrooms in different parts of the country and from all corners of the globe and are able to tap into resources and make connections anywhere in the world.

In the past, schools and the students within them existed in isolation. Foreign countries and cultures were things that could be explored only through reference books—books usually written by people who lived far, far away from the places they were writing about. This education was strictly a one-way exchange, as well. Students would read a book and consume the information contained within, but the learning stopped there. There was no way for them to ask questions, go deeper, or develop any sort of feeling of understanding or empathy about the people who lived in these places. From time to time, classes would take field trips to local attractions or museums. This might even include trips to cities or landmarks hundreds of miles away.

For example, trips to Washington, DC, for eighth graders were commonplace. Many affluent schools sponsored trips overseas. But these were short-lived and often one-sided—tour guides and docents provided information, with little opportunity for students to truly interact or immerse themselves in the different location or culture.

This is no longer the case. Thanks to the Internet and other technologies, a global approach is just a click away. In fact, the concept of "global" has all but ceased to exist. Even the farthest reaches of the planet are "local," in a sense. Antarctic explorers tweet and host webcasts. Students in Asia build websites and produce videos with students in the United States. World leaders communicate via YouTube videos, and students everywhere can do the same. With the click of a mouse, students can have live conversations with friends in different parts of the country. With just a small amount of teaching, students can build collaborative projects and reports with students on the other side of the globe. Such collaboration is happening as we speak in classrooms across the country, but it needs to start happening on a wider scale.

Education and the Global Economy

The reasons globally connected schools need to increase in number are many. The number of jobs requiring work across distances is increasing, making it clear that schools must prepare students for a vastly different workplace than in the past.

A flattened, globally connected workplace in the world that our current students will enter will be the norm, *not* the exception. These students will be expected to compete and thrive in an environment where working with someone 10,000 miles away is as common as working with a company down the block. This requires a unique and deep skill set. Students cannot be expected to develop these skills on their own. Schools owe it to their students to prepare them for the world of work that awaits them.

Unfortunately, as Tony Wagner (2010) writes, American schools are not keeping up. He argues that even the most high-performing schools aren't promoting what he calls the "Seven Survival Skills" that are essential for career readiness in the 21st century:

- Critical Thinking and Problem Solving
- Collaboration Across Networks
- Agility and Adaptability

- Initiative and Entrepreneurship
- Effective Oral and Written Communication
- Accessing and Analyzing Information
- Curiosity and Imagination

(p.67)

Without these skills, U.S. graduates cannot compete in the global economy.

Obviously, the primary function of K-12 education is to prepare students for the world after school. Are educators not obligated, then, to help develop this skill set in students? Every student who enters the workforce *not* knowing how to connect and collaborate across distances enters at a distinct competitive disadvantage.

What can schools do? Our description of Shift 2 will answer that question in detail to provide a step-by-step approach for how a broader emphasis on global collaboration can occur. This starts on a classroom and school level, where students are taught the skills essential to collaboration. Then expansion occurs as connections are made outside the school and classrooms collaborate on projects. Continued expansion, with multiple classes in multiple locations involved, follows next—until your classroom is no longer simply a part of your own school building, but part of a larger educational enterprise—the global classroom.

Global Citizenship

Educators aren't preparing students for just the workforce and the global economy, however. Global citizenship, a phrase we use to describe the way students interact with the world and the positive impact they make upon it, is of the utmost importance. Understanding the world and demonstrating empathy toward different cultures are key components of the concept of global citizenship.

Here is a more detailed definition of this concept, created by Oxfam (1997):

We see a Global Citizen as someone who:

- is aware of the wider world and has a sense of their own role as a world citizen

- respects and values diversity
- has an understanding of how the world works economically, politically, socially, culturally, technologically and environmentally
- is outraged by social injustice
- participates in and contributes to the community at a range of levels from local to global
- is willing to act to make the world a more sustainable place
- takes responsibility for their actions.

(p.3)

How can these characteristics be better emphasized in school? A fundamental shift needs to happen. You won't find these standards in a Common Core State Standards (CCSS) document or on a standardized test, and that's why the idea of citizenship easily slips through the cracks of the teaching day. But in today's world, it is imperative that this doesn't happen.

Imagine the possibilities of a globally connected classroom. Think of all that your students could learn and accomplish as you guide them to explore and connect with the world around them. Global experiences are worthwhile for both teachers and students. They must be a key component of modern education. As Davis and Lindsay (2012) write: "We need this connection for the future of the planet. It is no longer an option." Global is, after all, the new local. In Chapter 5, you'll read our detailed steps to implementing a global classroom, and in Chapter 6, we'll share some of our own stories to help inspire and assist you in taking the steps to global collaboration.

Summary

- Global is the new local—information, resources, and connections from distant locales are made available with a click of the mouse in the 21st century.
- The ever-changing global economy will demand collaboration skills that should be provided by K-12 educators.
- Global citizenship should be a major focus of our work as modern educators.

Implementation

The energy that bubbles within a globally connected classroom is palpable, and the excitement of building a global classroom is immeasurable. By making a commitment to connect your classroom or school to the world outside its walls, you are embarking upon an exciting adventure. It is an adventure that may possibly be fraught with challenges. You may find setbacks and even failures. However, every experience along the way will have educational value, and the end result has the potential to transcend everything you ever thought was possible about teaching and learning while making a lasting impact on the lives of students.

In this chapter, we will explore a series of steps designed to help you make the shift from a classroom that exists on a local level, to one that has "gone global." These include the following:

- Teaching the skills essential for global collaboration
- Engaging in "local" projects
- Finding an established global project
- Forming a personal learning network and leveraging Twitter to make connections
- Connecting through established social networking forums
- Designing DIY global projects
- Empowering global citizens

In the interest of clarity, it is important that educators know what outcomes they are seeking. A global classroom is one that features all the following:

- Connections and communications between schools via Skype and other technologies such as wikis, blogs, or e-mail
- Collaboration with other schools to work on common assignments
- Creation of learning artifacts, with work shared among all students

How does an effective global classroom become established? It is certainly not an overnight process, and it begins with a commitment from a dedicated educator like yourself. Here are five steps for educators interested in creating a global classroom or school.

Step 1: Develop Habits of Collaboration

Starting small is key when endeavoring to connect your classroom to schools in other locations. Jumping right into a global project without first developing some important foundational habits in your students might lead to frustration for them and to your own conclusion that global connections just "aren't for you." Before reaching out to the world, look first within the soon-to-be-flattened walls of your own classroom and ask yourself if you and your students are ready.

Consider for a moment what you're ultimately attempting to do—connect, collaborate, and create with students from different time zones, states, cultures, and countries. Within the classroom, you will facilitate the connections. In the 21st-century classroom, students' production and creation of evidence of high-level learning is not unique. (See Shift 1 of this book for more details about how to make this happen.) However, the habits of effective collaboration may not be second nature for your students. These habits, like those of so many other traditional school subjects, such as reading, writing, and arithmetic, must be taught first. That's why you're there, after all. Before taking your students' work onto the global stage, though, consider all that is entailed in collaboration. There are several skills that people must possess in order to truly collaborate, and those skills should all be explicitly taught. Though this involves some work for you on the front end of the collaborative process, if you are truly interested in developing this critical skill, it will prove to be time well spent. The processes and protocols we outline will be used over and over by your students throughout the school year and, we hope, beyond. This method will help these collaborative skills become ingrained habits for your students.

Following are three key collaboration skills that must be developed prior to starting on meaningful and effective collaborative projects.

Brainstorming

Brainstorming sessions, an essential part of any collaborative endeavor, seem like straightforward tasks, but when brainstorming skills are not explicitly taught, sessions intended to give all participants a voice and help groups share the responsibility of finding the best option can quickly turn into a maelstrom of conflict and disagreement.

To teach brainstorming is to teach a protocol, a protocol that includes clear expectations, or norms, of each member of the group. What follows is our proposed protocol for brainstorming—notice that each step has a fairly strict time limit. We all know that time is a valuable resource, but it is critical to help students realize this, too, from the very beginning.

1. Assign Roles (*one minute*)

   You will need a facilitator to keep time and enforce the protocol and a recorder to capture everyone's ideas.

2. Review Norms (*one minute*)

   There are two critical expectations of all members: no judgment and no negativity. This is not the time to critique one another's ideas. That's for a later time.

3. Pose First Question and Begin Brainstorming (*ten minutes*)

   During this portion, go around the group, with each member sharing one idea. Each idea is recorded. Any member who does not have an idea may pass. Again, no commentary or criticism of any ideas is allowed.

Repeat number 3, depending upon how many questions have been posed to the group.

This protocol serves two purposes. It empowers students to share any and all ideas, from the basic to the creative and kooky. It also keeps students focused on the most important part of brainstorming: ideas! The key in setting up a brainstorming session in this way is to project a more-the-merrier attitude about ideas, and with everyone encouraged to have a voice there should be no shortage of ideas. However, remember that this is a process that has to be taught and that students need ample scaffolding and practice time. Once they've mastered the process, though, your class is on its way to functioning like a well-oiled machine.

Making Decisions

In the same vein as brainstorming, the collaborative decision-making process is something that should be taught like any other skill, something that students need to practice in order to master. Once groups have brainstormed a thorough list of ideas, the list must be narrowed and a final decision reached. This brings discussion into the process for the first time, and the key with this step is to explicitly teach students how to productively make decisions without passing judgment.

How do you do this? It is a good idea, again, to set up a protocol for students to follow. Think first, though, about what you want them to accomplish. Ideally, you want them, on their own, to narrow down a list of ideas and choose the one they believe is best. You want this to happen without arguments, hostility, or hard feelings. Fear not; it can be done.

1. Determine Roles *(one minute)*

   This time, each group needs a facilitator, a timekeeper, and a note taker. The facilitator moves the group from one idea to the next. The timekeeper watches the clock, and the note-taker records everyone's thoughts.

2. Review Norms *(one minute)*

   These are the same as in the brainstorming protocol: no judgment and no negativity.

3. Ask for Silent Reflection *(five minutes)*

   Spend a moment during which everyone in the group peruses the list and thinks about what ideas are best and why. The key word here is *ideas*, as each member should try to find more than one.

4. Share with the Group *(five minutes)*

   Each member of the group shares one idea he or she likes best, explaining its good points. More than one group member can share the same idea, but be sure everyone's reasons are recorded.

5. Eliminate Ideas *(one minute)*

   Any idea not mentioned is removed.

6. Select *(five to ten minutes)*

   Make a final selection by reaching consensus on the best overall option.

Being Accountable

Accountability is a critical part of collaboration that can be boiled down to three essential questions: What do we need to do? Who is going to do what? When is the project going to be done? This skill doesn't need a protocol, but your students will benefit from learning how to answer these questions. Explaining to students what "accountability" looks like, perhaps with a role play, will help them in their own work.

1. What Do We Have to Do to Accomplish the Goal/Project We Decided Upon?

   List the steps, and discuss what the finished product will look like. Being explicit with the outcomes you expect is key. Also key is that students do most of the work in defining the outcomes. This gives them a sense of ownership and deepens their investment in their work. (You'll find much more on the value of student choice in Chapters 10–12.)

2. Who Is Going to Take Which Part?

   We hope students can determine this on their own. Working through the difficult decisions of this step can be tricky, but if all students have contributed ideas and shared during the previous step, everyone will have at least one task of interest.

3. When Does Each Part Need to Be Finished?

   Students should understand the importance of this step. The key is for students to feel accountable to one another, not just to their teacher. Often during group work, a situation arises in which one student takes over, assuming many or all of the group's responsibilities. This leads to resentment and dysfunction, as well as an overworked leader and a group of students who are skating by without holding up their end of the bargain.

   None of these things takes a great deal of time to teach. However, a deliberate and intentional approach toward developing these basic skills will pay off in the long run, and once they are developed, students can transfer the skills into every collaborative situation they find themselves in, both within school and in the world of work.

One concern many teachers raise at this point is "How do I make this fit into my already tight schedule? My plate is full with testing, standards, and countless other requirements." Our response is simple: If you are looking to build a globally collaborative classroom, these skills are vital. Look for ways to incorporate them into the standards-based work you are already doing. Chances are, group work is something you're already using with students. Taking a few moments to implement these practices and build these collaborative skills will only serve to improve it—without getting in the way of meeting standards and other requirements. (For more insight on how global projects can meet CCSS, see Chapter 6.)

Step 2: Before Going Global, Go Local

Now that your students are well versed in the skill of collaboration, having developed them within the confines of your own classroom, it is time to expand their reach—not too far, though. In keeping with our baby-step approach to going global, Step 2 involves putting these habits to the test during collaborative activities with other classes in your own school. Sure, it can be great to jump right into a project with a school in another state or country, but by starting your work with a colleague or friend at your school, you improve your chances of success when you start collaborating with strangers. Here are some benefits of a local collaboration:

Student Familiarity

Working with students your students already know adds an element of comfort to collaborative project work. It's easy for many of us to work with people we do not know, but remember that not everyone feels that same level of social comfort. By easing into collaborative projects with people they know, students are better prepared to take risks, speak up, listen to others, and take ownership of their work. All these are key components of global collaborative projects, and all of them are best developed in an environment in which students share at least a school in common, if not more.

Teacher Familiarity

Just as working with people they don't know can be intimidating for students, the same can be true for teachers. Trying out new approaches or practices is a daunting task, and collaborative projects require a great deal of planning for the teachers involved. Undertaking such projects also requires bravery, boldness, and confidence on a teacher's part. It can be much easier to become all of these things when you are working in tandem with a teacher or teachers you know already. You may make mistakes, have confusion, and experience failures (all of which are inevitable—more on this in a moment), but with familiar colleagues, you will find these failings much less debilitating and more manageable.

Common Curriculum

One of the challenges of working with schools in other parts of the country or world is creating work that aligns to different standards and curricula. Ideally, your global project will address requirements of all classrooms involved. Whether these are content expectations, CCSS, or any other requirements involving different curricula, working with differences among these things can pose a challenge. This isn't to say that the challenge is insurmountable; it isn't, and we'll talk more about this later in this section. However, just as familiarity removes several barriers in your early collaborative work, working within your own school on your first collaborative efforts removes the barrier of different curricula. Within your school, teachers are working toward the same end, and you're using a common curriculum and standards. This leads to an easier time planning and executing collaborative projects. Save the curriculum challenges for later, when you're better versed in all it takes to pull off a collaborative project.

This initial collaborative effort does not have to involve a long-term project. It can, of course, but a short series of collaborative activities over the course of a few class periods can be equally beneficial. Furthermore, it does not have to involve the creation of anything new. Look for ways to collaborate on activities you're already planning to do. For example, if you and another teacher are teaching the same science (or math, social studies, etc.) unit, why not combine forces and create lab groups with students from both classes? This builds those essential collaborative skills and provides practice for future collaborative ventures.

Another thought to keep in mind is to create situations in which students can practice the skills they've worked on during habit-building activities in Step 1: brainstorming, decision making, and accountability. Be sure to include these in your local collaborative work.

Here are three other ways you can easily design collaborative work for students in the same grade and/or area of study. Despite being general in nature, they are sure to help jump-start your collaborative efforts.

Open-Ended Questions

This can work in nearly every part of the day. The key is to ask your collaborative groups a question that has more than one answer or more than one way to arrive at the answer. You could even ask a question that has no known answer! You could ask a question about language arts (Which character in these three books was most dynamic?) or science (Is there life on other planets?) or social studies (Which Native American tribe was forced to overcome the most adversity?). Mathematics provides a terrific opportunity for collaboration as well. A multistep word problem or performance task can be challenging and exciting for students to work on together.

This method also presents the opportunity to combine multiple subject areas. For example, the seemingly innocuous yet challenging question "How do you measure a puddle?" combines math and science and can yield some very creative responses.

No matter which discipline your open-ended question focuses on, you'll find that it presents engaging and meaningful ways for students to collaborate in an effort to develop an answer.

A Challenge

We've all been to workshops with team-building icebreakers or similar kickoff activities. These can range from exciting to mundane, although it's often the latter. However, a well-designed challenge can really help students build collaborative skills.

Have students take the "Marshmallow Challenge," described by Tom Wujec in his TED Talk, "Build a Tower, Build a Team" (Wujec, 2010). Wujec discusses a challenge that involves teams attempting to build the tallest tower they can using only dry spaghetti, one yard of tape, and one marshmallow in only 18 minutes.

This challenge doesn't have much curricular relevance, but it will go a long way toward building collaboration skills.

Digital Collaborative Tools

An effectively designed global project should require students to use digital tools that are well suited for collaboration. A great way to familiarize students with the tools in this stage is to have them practice using them in collaborative activities with fellow classmates or students in other classes within your own school. That way, the global project isn't their first experience, and your students are already well prepared to use them.

Here are some digital tools and suggested uses for them in a same-school collaborative setting:

Skype

A Skype call can be an exhilarating experience for students, especially young ones. However, the thrill can be overwhelming the first time you try it and can lead to an unfocused discussion or outright silliness, neither of which is conducive to collaboration!

Why not set up a call with another class within your own school to help practice Skype norms? This would give students a chance to get used to speaking loudly enough and paying attention to the speaker. It also eases the excitement of a new experience. All of this will help your first real Skype call to be a success. Ahead of time, the teachers can choose a focus—perhaps a book or poem that was read aloud to both classes or a primary source that was explored in both American history classes.

Google Drive

Using Google Drive (drive.google.com), students can work collaboratively on a Google Document or Spreadsheet. This collaboration can happen in real time or asynchronously (at different times), with students from both classes entering text or data from different computers.

Wikis

Wikis (collaborative websites) are very simple to use. Students from different classes can build a wiki together about a shared learning goal or topic.

Edmodo

Edmodo is a safe and secure social network designed specifically for educational settings. With Edmodo, a teacher creates a group and then provides a code that allows students to join the group. As a way of developing networking and communication skills, the students who are working together can exchange posts and comments via an Edmodo group.

Step 3: Join Existing Global Projects

If you've completed the previous two steps, you and your students are definitely ready to take the plunge into a global project. Davis and Lindsay (2012), founders of the Flat Classroom series of global collaborative projects, offer terrific advice for teachers who find themselves ready to begin this endeavor: "Don't reinvent the wheel." They suggest resisting the urge to start something from scratch on your own, but instead start by joining an already-existing project.

The benefits of beginning this way are numerous, but the two chief ones include removing the design element and eliminating the legwork involved in making your own connections with other schools. When you join an existing project, it already has been created, so you won't have to think of a new idea, one that will interest others and contain all the elements of a successful project. Furthermore, you won't have to make connections with other teachers around the world. This step involves a great deal of time and effort (and can often yield disappointing results). The good news is that there is no shortage of projects you can join in which the connections with other schools are made for you by project facilitators. This lessens your workload and increases the probability of a successful project. Some of the best existing projects include the following:

The Flat Classroom Project
(www.flatclassroomproject.net)

This group of projects, created by the aforementioned Davis and Lindsay, provides opportunities for teachers in grades kindergarten through 12 to interact and collaborate with students across the country and around the world. These projects have been developed with creation in mind—students collaborate across time zones to create videos, websites, blogs, and more.

Over the years, the Flat Classroom has expanded from the original project, which explores the impact of technology on our society, to include other projects, including Digiteen (a study of digital citizenship), NetGenEd (an exploration of the future of education and social action), and Eracism (an online research project and debate designed to promote awareness of racism and other societal challenges). All these projects are designed for secondary-age students. Recently added to this suite of projects are the "A Week in the Life" project for grades 3 through 5 and "Building Bridges to Tomorrow" for kindergarten through grade 2. All the above projects run twice per school year.

Challenge 20/20 (www.nais.org/Articles/Pages/
Challenge-20-20.aspx)

Created and managed by the National Association of Independent Schools (NAIS), Challenge 20/20 partners U.S. and global schools around the common goal of brainstorming solutions to the world's 20 most challenging problems. These global problems are based on the book *High Noon: 20 Global Problems, 20 Years to Solve Them*, by Jean-François Rischard, and range from water scarcity and climate change to biotechnology and peacekeeping and international terrorism.

After a brief application process, NAIS partners schools that are interested in common issues. Applications are due in the late summer, and the project runs twice per year. Challenge 20/20 is completely free and open to all schools, private and public, and all grades, from kindergarten through 12.

The Global Read Aloud (www.globalreadaloud.com)

Started in 2010 by Wisconsin educator Pernille Ripp, the Global Read Aloud takes place each fall for students in elementary grades. The project, which is free and includes more than 30,000 students, involves teachers reading aloud a common book within their own classrooms and then collaborating via online discussions and other creative endeavors, such as digital movies, slideshows, and more.

This project is slightly different from the previous two in that classes are not partnered with other classrooms; teachers work on their own to make connections and share student work with other participants. Fortunately, the large number of classrooms that take part makes this process quite easy. The Global Read Aloud is an exciting experience and one that helps students develop a meaningful understanding of the importance of global connections and cultural understanding.

The Global Virtual Classroom (gvc-clubhouse.wikispaces.com)

The GVC, a website sponsored by the organization Give Something Back International (www.gsbi.org), is a unique option for teachers seeking global connections. GVC doesn't feature projects but, through its "Clubhouse" wiki page, facilitates connections between schools. After submitting an application, your class is partnered with a school from around the world. From there, the teachers involved work together to determine what form their projects will take.

iEARN (www.iearn.org)

The International Education and Research Network (iEARN) has been working to help schools collaborate since well before the digital age. Established in 1988, iEARN enables educators from around the globe to connect via their Project Collaboration Centre. Within this online group are 150 projects, created by people from more than one hundred countries. Once you register, you can find a project that suits your classroom's profile and your students' academic needs.

The Value of Intra-national Connections

Connecting with classrooms in other countries can be incredibly exciting, but don't discount the value of connecting with schools in other states or even within your own. There is much value in connecting with local communities. Your students will still develop collaborative skills. It will reduce the issues caused by time zones, which makes it easier to schedule real time interactions. Finally, within the United States, vast cultural differences exist that students can discover and explore. A class in inner-city Chicago that connects with a class in rural Alabama will be able to learn about and value the differences between two communities that are a part of the same nation. This can lead to valuable learning opportunities.

Step 4: Use Social Networks to Create Your Own Projects

At this point, you may be content with your work. You have joined one or more existing projects and are pleased with the successes you and your students have accomplished. Welcome to the world of global collaboration!

Some educators, however, find themselves itching for more at this point. Having participated in some projects, they now have ideas of their own, and their thoughts turn to building a project themselves. Though this can be a challenging process involving tremendous legwork both in designing a project and making connections, the rewards for you and your students far outweigh the drawbacks. Once you've got a project idea, the key is to take it public and broadcast it to the masses in hopes of making connections with other educators. This takes a combination of courage and intelligence: courage because you're taking your idea out into the world and sharing it with educators from around the world; intelligence because if you don't publicize your project in the proper forums, no one will ever find it, and it will fizzle before it even starts.

How can you make this happen? Again, there is no need to completely start from scratch. Several existing networks boast memberships in the tens of thousands (or more) of educators. Wisely using these can lead to meaningful connections and exciting collaborative opportunities. Here are a few networks that can serve as excellent starting points:

Classroom 2.0 (www.classroom20.com)

An online network for teachers founded by educational technology thought leader Steve Hargadon, Classroom 2.0 boasts a membership of more than 70,000 educators from all over the world. The network features discussion forums and groups where members can post project ideas and requests for partnerships. For example, if you are an elementary teacher, you can join the Elementary group and post your project idea. Other members can email you or reply to your post if they want to collaborate with you.

Global Education Conference Network (www. globaleducationconference.com)

This network is designed for teachers interested in global education. Co-founded by Steve Hargadon and educational consultant Lucy Gray, the GEC Network has more than 15,000 members and uses the same type of platform as Classroom 2.0. Teachers connect through this site, leading to exciting collaborative projects. Also worth noting is the actual Global Education Conference itself, which is held each November. This online conference is completely free and features educators from around the world presenting about issues and ideas regarding global education.

Skype in the Classroom (education.skype.com)

Skype has built an impressive network for educators interested in collaboration. Teachers can search for projects designed by other educators and also post their own creations. A Skype account is required, but the site is completely free. Your project will be posted publicly for thousands of teachers to access. Projects are searchable by geographic location, age and grade level, and subject.

Twitter

Some of the best collaborative projects begin on Twitter. A strong Twitter network can lead to meaningful connections with other educators. Once your project has been designed and you're looking for partners, simply tweet about your idea and ask for interested teachers to get in touch with you. Obviously, the more Twitter followers you have, the more people there are who will see your project proposal. To increase the number of educators who see your tweets, use hashtags, searchable keywords that are preceded by the pound (#) sign. One hashtag that is widely followed is #globaled. Another is #edchat. There are also hashtags for grade levels, such as #5thchat and #4thchat, and subject areas, such as #mathchat and #engchat. Using an appropriate hashtag can lead to much better results than sending a tweet without one. Because of the nature of Twitter, though, you may have to tweet multiple times over a series of days or weeks. Your persistence will pay off, and it won't be long before teachers are getting in touch with you to collaborate. (You can read more about Twitter in Shift 5 of this book, "Isolated Versus Connected.")

Failure: Definitely an Option

Unfortunately, not every project turns into a roaring success. For every Flat Classroom project—a project that starts as a grassroots experiment and turns into a runaway hit—there are many projects that fizzle. This can happen for any number of reasons, but it's important to recognize it as a possibility. Don't be discouraged about giving your project a try, however. Each attempt can be a learning experience, and each time you try it, it will get better. Here are some tips, based upon our experiences, that might help ensure a successful project:

It's in the Details

An attention to detail as you design your project is critical. A project with clear deadlines and expectations, laid out in advance for all participants to see, has many benefits. It will help potential partners understand all that the project will entail and all that will be expected of their students. In essence, it lets them know what they're getting into. It's easy to think that a we'll-see-where-this-goes-and-play-it-by-ear attitude can work. But you will increase the odds of success by planning out everything and being explicit about the expectations, objectives, outcomes, and deadlines in advance.

Home Base

Your project needs a home, a permanent place on the Web, where everyone can access the project details and requirements. This can be a blog, a wiki, or any other type of page. Without a home, or by relying only on email and document attachments, it's easy for other teachers to get lost along the way.

Face Time

Once you have enlisted other teachers to participate, it is a good idea to schedule an online meeting via webinar, Skype, or Google Hangout. This will help forge a bond among you and your partners. It's a great way to get to know one another, and it also adds a sense of "reality" to your project. The teachers you are working with become real people, rather than email addresses or online entities. When you know each other and connect face-to-face (even virtually), it adds an element of accountability. The participants will work harder to make sure your project is a success because they've gotten to know one another. Scheduling regular online meetings throughout the project is a good idea, too, as a way of maintaining the connections and keeping everyone informed and making sure they have a chance to reflect and adjust.

What Have We Learned?

- Before beginning a collaborative project with other schools, developing habits of collaboration within your own classroom, including brainstorming, decision making, and accountability, is a good idea.
- Practicing collaboration with other classrooms within your own school can be beneficial before attempting to work with teachers elsewhere.

- Existing, established collaborative projects are a great starting point because they are well organized and able to facilitate the hardest part of global collaboration—making connections.

- When you are ready to design your own project, there are several places to get the word out to attract participants.

- Failure may occur, but you can take steps to minimize the risk that it will occur.

What Now?

You're ready to shift your focus from local to global. Here are some ways you can do that, arranged by skill level.

NOVICE:
Work with a colleague to transform an activity you already have planned into something more collaborative. Find ways to combine your classes and examine how you can teach students to work and learn together. Build in time to develop habits of collaboration. Allow students to work collaboratively to meet your learning outcomes.

INTERMEDIATE:
Join an existing collaborative project such as the Flat Classroom Project or Challenge 20/20. Be sure to take part in the pre-project planning sessions with your teaching partners so you develop a relationship with them. Work as your students' guide, letting them take on the challenging work themselves as you support them. Celebrate your accomplishments at the conclusion of the project!

EXPERT:
Design your own collaborative project. Reach out through social networks such as Twitter, Classroom 2.0, Skype in the Classroom, and the Global Education Conference network to find collaborative partners. Remember: a well-designed and organized project has a higher chance of success. Also, patience and persistence are necessary when attempting to make connections. If your first attempts aren't successful, keep trying.

Anecdotes

We made a commitment to "going global" with our classrooms a few years ago. Always looking for new ways to engage our students in meaningful learning activities and to instill in them the traits of 21st-century learners, we decided that global collaborative projects would be excellent ways to do both these things. They would enable us to take part in and design work that did all of that *and* was aligned to teaching standards.

In this chapter, we will share some of our own experiences. We hope these, combined with the steps outlined in the previous chapter, will inspire you to "go global" yourself.

Water Scarcity and Challenge 20/20

Challenge 20/20 (described in more detail in Chapter 5) is a project that connects classrooms in an effort to empower students to collaborate to solve the world's twenty biggest problems. Our classrooms in Detroit, Michigan were partnered with a school in Southern California and a school in Kuwait with the challenge of exploring the topic of water scarcity. These partnerships were established by the organizers of the project, the National Association of Independent Schools (NAIS).

Our work began with an organizational meeting. The three schools connected via Skype to discuss our options. A great part of this project was that though the topic was assigned to us (but you do get to rank your preferences on the application), the design and the outcomes were left to us. The teachers involved were able to plan the project and decide what the final product would look like. When we met (midday East Coast time, so no one had to get up in the middle of the night!), we created an outline of what we would do: challenge students to create projects that would teach them, and students everywhere in the world, about the water issues that were specific to our own regions.

As you can imagine, the issues of water scarcity vary dramatically in these three locations. It was exciting to think about empowering our students to do the teaching of a fairly complicated topic.

As a group, the teachers wanted to add an element of collaboration and discussion to the project as well, so we set up an Edmodo group for students to ask one another questions, both about what they were learning and about the work they shared. The feedback students received in this group worked as a helpful way for them to revise and improve their work. Imagine creating a slideshow to teach students thousands of miles away about water issues in your region and then sharing the lesson with those students, who in turn ask questions and provide feedback so students can return to their work and improve it. As an example, there were groups in our classrooms who hadn't explained what the Great Lakes were and where they were located. In the Edmodo group, another student commented on this and suggested adding maps to the slideshow so the geography would make sense to viewers unfamiliar with the region—tremendous (and helpful!) feedback for a fourth grader. The fact that it came from a peer in Kuwait served to deepen the impact.

The final products ended up being brilliant and informative, and the entire learning experience was invaluable.

Book Club 2.0: An Exploration of Literature

Challenge 20/20 was an existing, established project, but we also wanted to try our hand at creating our own collaborative project. After a great deal of brainstorming, we decided to build a project around books that would be read aloud to the participating classes. We are always looking for ways to integrate more reading and writing, as well as student discussion, into our teaching, and this seemed like an engaging way to do so.

We started by setting up a wiki for the book club. This served as the home page of the project, a place for us to post a timeline and discussion questions, along with student work that was created along the way. Then we selected a book for the first round (our hope was that this project could continue throughout the school year, with different classes choosing the book each time—just like a book club that meets in your living room!). At this point, it was time to connect with other teachers.

We reached out using several of the networks described in Chapter 5, including Classroom 2.0 and the Global Education Conference Network. We also emailed classes that had taken part in the Global Read Aloud (see Chapter 5 for details on this, as well). This was quite a leap of faith for us. We weren't really sure what would happen. We patiently waited for responses to come in—and they did. Our idea of different classrooms reading the same book aloud and then connecting online to discuss them seemed to resonate with other teachers.

For the first round of the club, using the book *The Maze of Bones*, by Rick Riordan, we were joined by classes from many different states, including Texas, Alabama, Colorado, and Georgia. Again, as a means of connecting, we chose Edmodo. Teachers posted questions and polls for students to answer, and students not only replied but also eventually began to ask one another questions. Along the way, teachers were able to teach important skills, such as how to write a meaningful answer to a question and how to ask meaningful questions, questions that go deeper than "What was your favorite part?"

At different points in the book, classes also engaged in some digital activities, including podcasting and creating Glogs and VoiceThreads. These were shared via Edmodo so that other students could explore them and comment. At the end of the book, we were even able to schedule a live discussion with one of the participants. For the first time ever for our students, we took part in a Skype call with a partner class in suburban Atlanta, Georgia. Students found this an incredibly thrilling and meaningful learning experience. They explored a 21st-century communication method, one that will be a ubiquitous fixture in the world of work they will enter after leaving school.

The club continued for two more rounds, reading the books *Regarding the Fountain*, by Kate Klise, and *Love That Dog*, by Sharon Creech. In a stroke of serendipity, the book club even received an email from Klise, thanking us for taking an interest in her book, praising our work, and encouraging us to keep reading books of all kinds!

We noted several things during this experience:

Student Engagement and Motivation

Students were excited and engaged throughout this work. They were invested, which was one of our goals. There was a great deal of intrinsic motivation at work here, too. Students *wanted* to do well. They begged for computer time to check their Edmodo posts. They worked furiously to meet deadlines so they could share their work with their online friends. They took time at home to log on and discuss the books. And they did all this on their own, without prodding. The work was exciting, the connections were meaningful, and students were fully invested in doing a good job— not because their teachers were encouraging them to do so, but because they wanted to themselves. We also noticed that students who were previously not very interested in reading or writing or were hesitant to participate in class discussions actively engaged and participated in a meaningful way.

Academic Content

This was not an exercise in "fluff," work that serves no purpose. Being able to think critically about a text, to ask good questions, and to write good answers were goals of the project, and all are important academic outcomes. And they were all achieved by our work here. Even just a brief look at the Common Core Anchor Standards for reading, writing, and speaking and listening reveals that several were addressed in our book club work, including those that call for close reading and answering questions using supporting textual evidence.

Technology Integration

In this experience, technology played a big role. However, its purpose was not superficial. The technology made the connections possible; it wasn't added for a "bells and whistles" effect. Without the technology, a project of this sort would not have been possible.

Social Media Practice

Edmodo operates as an alternative to Facebook, allowing students to engage in social media usage even if they are under 13, the minimum age for Facebook and other social media accounts. Why is this important? We owe it to our students to have frank discussions about social media use (and abuse) in schools and to provide them with safe ways of practicing social media skills—leaving quality comments, maintaining a level of respect even when disagreeing or questioning another's thoughts, etc. Furthermore, we have a responsibility to demonstrate the positive power of social media, including how it can bring people together and be used as a learning tool. This project did these things for all involved.

Exploration of Other Cultures

Our interest in global projects was born from a desire to help our students better understand the world around them. More specifically, we hoped to develop an awareness that a world beyond our local borders actually exists. Our students live isolated lives and attend a school that is monocultural. Diversity is not something they get to experience very much; they don't have the opportunity to go to school with students of other cultures. This leads to common misunderstandings, false conclusions, and a lack of understanding about the world in which they live. Essentially, what we were trying to do was open their eyes to the true nature of our planet—that it's a place of numerous cultures and ethnicities and that there is much to learn about places that are completely new to us.

We entered into a series of cultural exchanges with schools in three different countries: Taiwan, Turkey, and Russia. These connections were established through a short post we made in a Classroom 2.0 discussion group in which we sought out partner classrooms, as well as through connections made via the Global Virtual Classroom (gvc-clubhouse. wikispaces.com), an organization that facilitates global educational partnerships for teachers.

Our goal was simple—to answer this question for our global partners: "How can we teach people in other countries what life is like here?" Our friends in these partner countries set out to answer the same question for us.

Although this project did not involve a great deal of collaboration, it was designed to be as interactive as possible. Students traded emails and made one another slideshows about their native countries, sharing with them different customs, historical information, foods, and as much as possible helped provide an understanding of what life is like in these different places.

Our own students decided to focus on four different areas: life at school, life at home, things we like to do, and things we like to eat. Students worked together in small groups to gather images and write explanations to help their new friends understand the United States and its culture. After trading slideshows, students sent one another follow-up questions, asking more about what they'd seen. (One of our favorite questions came from Taiwan for the things-we-like-to-eat group: "Is your food always of this size?")

Through this work, students were able to learn a great deal more and have much more meaningful experiences than they would have had simply by reading books about Turkey, Russia, and Taiwan. We also engaged in meaningful discussions within our own classrooms about things that fascinated them, including the concepts of traditional dress and dance and the idea that there are buildings in countries like Turkey, Russia, and others that are older than any structures standing in our own country.

Tapping into students' natural curiosity was one of the many benefits of this exchange. All too often in schools, students are not encouraged to ask questions or to be curious, despite the fact that they are naturally inclined to do both of these things. They were able not only to ask questions but also to get answers from cultural experts—students actually living in these countries.

Students with C.L.A.S.S.

As our final anecdote, we are compelled to share a story that didn't directly involve us. It is an amazing global project created by teachers at the Prairie School in Racine, Wisconsin, and we are proud to say it was a project we played a part (albeit a minor one; the teachers there deserve all the credit) in helping to facilitate.

In the fall of 2011, we were contacted by Prairie fourth-grade teacher Chris Henke Mueller. Chris and her colleagues Sarah Barbian (middle school reading, French, ESL), Greg Gidden (U.S. history), and Dominic Inouye (U.S. English department chair) were looking to forge a connection with students in Afghanistan. They had established a connection the prior year, but due to circumstances beyond their control they had fallen out of touch with this group. We recommended the usual options and reached out to our own network of global education experts in an attempt to help. Unfortunately, every path seemed to lead to a dead end.

One day, we stumbled upon a site that seemed to fit their needs perfectly. Through the Global Connections and Exchange Program (gceafghanistan.ning.com), Chris and her team found a group to partner with for grades 4 through 10 in their program called C.L.A.S.S. (Character Leadership Accountability Sustainability Service).

The group spent a great deal of time on service-oriented projects within their own community. In addition, for four months, members of C.L.A.S.S. built a relationship with their partners in Jalalabad, Afghanistan. Through the use of a Ning website (a type of network designed for online communities), students traded posts, sharing ideas and learning about one another's cultures. As would be expected, deep bonds were formed, and in the spring, the classes were ready to meet face-to-face for the first time, via Skype. However, real life intervened, and schools in Jalalabad were closed following a violent protest and military crisis. Despite their concerns and fears (and a time zone challenge that had C.L.A.S.S. members reporting to school at 9:30 p.m., and their counterparts doing the same at 7:00 a.m. local time), the Skype call finally took place. Meeting face-to-face was a glorious moment for both groups of students, and one they are sure never to forget—just as they are sure to always maintain an understanding and deep appreciation for the people of a faraway country.

This was not an instance of collaboration around a shared work product or project but rather collaboration around a shared goal: cultural under-standing. The product of this collaboration became an increased sense of empathy for the community around them. In essence, their global work inspired them to do more locally. The group partnered with local organizations to help build awareness about hunger in their community. They also built a school garden to grow food for local food organizations and explored ways that urban gardening in the greater community could do the same. In addition, the students decided together that illiteracy was an issue that needed attention. So they partnered with another local school to find ways to shed light on literacy concerns as well as ways to help solve these problems together.

Their understanding about what it means to be human may not be measurable on a standardized test, but it is when you examine the work they accomplished, their enthusiasm and dedication, and their desire to make changes in the world. It's something that any group of students, in any place, is capable of. They just need guidance from dedicated and concerned adults.

"College and Career Ready" via Collaborative Projects

The explicit goal of the Common Core State Standards is to create an educational system that produces "students that are college and career ready." In the standards for English and Language Arts (National Governors Association Center for Best Practices, Council of Chief State School Officers, 2010), college- and career-ready students are described using the following set of criteria:

1. They are independent.
2. They build strong content knowledge.
3. They respond to the varying demands of audience, task, purpose, and discipline.
4. They comprehend as well as critique.
5. They value evidence.
6. They use technology and digital media strategically and capably.
7. They come to understand other perspectives and cultures.

Every one of these goals can become part of a collaborative project. It is almost as if the criteria were written with these types of projects in mind! Your work in shifting toward a global classroom is supported by the CCSS. Don't let the fear of meeting standards get in the way of making this shift. Instead, use your knowledge of what the standards do and do not say to build an effective rationale and a foundation for your work.

These four examples demonstrate how a dedication to global connections and collaboration can reap enormous dividends. Making global connections not only provides practice for the world of work that lays ahead for students but also develops a sense of global and cultural understanding and an understanding of students' place in the world. It can also inspire students to become agents of change.

It takes quite a leap of faith to make this shift in your classroom. It requires faith in teachers you've never met, faith in your students to take on the challenge, and faith in yourself. Global collaboration is a worthwhile challenge, however—one that can create lasting change in your students and in the world.

Shift 3: Searching Versus Filtering

An Introduction

Our third shift explores the changes from merely searching for information to filtering excess information. Today's 24-hour cable news, smartphones in every pocket, and the Internet in every classroom can easily lead to information overload. Instead of being hard to find information, it is now hard to figure out which information is accurate and useful. This, however, is a good problem to have.

We'll begin this shift by examining these areas:

- Previously, the challenge was merely locating information.
- Now, with information so abundant, the challenge is filtering useful information from the inaccurate and irrelevant.

Then, in Chapters 8 and 9, we will do the following:

- Show you how to move students from searching to filtering
- Provide you with examples of filtering activities

Locating Information

Before the Internet, finding good information was challenging. Any project that needed information, whether it be for school or something else, always involved going to the library or finding someone with knowledge of a subject. If you were lucky enough to live in a city with a large, useful public library, this wasn't usually too painful. It meant giving up only a weeknight evening or a weekend morning, driving to the library, flipping through the card catalog (literally), and trying to use the Dewey decimal system—only to have the book you really needed checked out or misplaced. This activity, which shouldn't have been very painful, grew increasingly more frustrating the more times it played out.

Perhaps, however, the information you needed couldn't be found in a book. Perhaps you wanted to find out about a local parade. You wanted to know when it was to be held, where the parade route was, who the grand marshal would be, why he or she was chosen as the grand marshal, etc. You wouldn't find the answers to those questions through a trip to the library. If you were very lucky and patient, an article in the local newspaper might come out at some point with answers to some of your questions. What if those answers didn't come miraculously via the paperboy? What next? Time to start calling people. First, try that neighbor of yours who knows everything about everything—no luck. Next, try calling city hall. If you're lucky enough for someone to answer, that person might tell you when the parade was happening and who the grand marshal was. A series of phone calls to various people and organizations might or might not eventually provide you with the answers you were looking for.

Finally, think about the issue of finding primary source material: original documents or firsthand accounts. Primary sources provide readers with unfiltered, unedited evidence. The phrase "Put your John Hancock here" makes a lot more sense after seeing the U.S. Declaration of Independence. In case you missed it, John Hancock signed his name bigger than anyone else did. You might have missed it because it wasn't easy to visit the Declaration of Independence. As we'll discuss later, the Declaration of Independence is now only a few keystrokes away.

A realistic assignment in November would be exploring the history of Thanksgiving. The best most students could do was find some second- or third-hand account of Squanto and the Pilgrims celebrating a bountiful harvest. By reading these accounts, however, it is difficult to decipher author biases, stereotypes, folklore, etc. Unless students were scholars of a given subject, people were forced to believe what they read. The opportunity to read primary sources was virtually nonexistent outside the world of scholars. As we moved from an era of searching to an era of filtering, this all began to change.

Filtering Information

The problems just detailed seem painfully trivial. If you were born after the mid-1980s, these problems might seem ridiculously inconceivable. With the introduction of the Internet, all the information in the world is at the tips of our fingers. The card catalog is now an online database that can be searched just as easily from home as at the library. Furthermore, it is possible to search the card catalog of nearly any library in the world from that same computer.

The problems of the parade can probably be solved with a simple Internet search or two. The parade time, route, and grand marshal are probably all listed on the city webpage. There may be a blog post from a local resident giving all the inside tips about the best places to sit on the route and when to get there. Wikipedia might have an article about the grand marshal. Plus you may be able to friend him or her on Facebook and follow her or him on Twitter.

The Internet, for better or worse, has brought primary sources to the masses. Anyone who wants to be can be a reporter. It is possible to take virtual trips down most major streets in the world. Many museums offer virtual tours of many of their exhibits. The Library of Congress has a whole Web page dedicated to primary sources (www.loc.gov/teachers). A Google search of "Put your John Hancock here" yields more than a million and a half results. Most of these websites do not contain primary sources, but they point you in the right direction. After reading about how that saying came from the Declaration of Independence, a logical next step would be to search for that document on Google Images. That search provides more than five and a half million images, most of which are of the primary source. The U.S. National Archives and Records Administration (www.archives.gov), where the document is physically housed, also provides high-resolution images of the front and back of the document, along with a typed transcript of the document to assist in reading it. And although the primary source has faded, it is still easy to see John Hancock's signature written across the bottom of the document.

A similar dissection of the primary sources related to the first Thanksgiving provides unfiltered views of this historical time. The Library of Congress, as mentioned earlier, provides hints to primary sources dealing with versions of Thanksgiving nearly 70 years before the Pilgrims'. Further digging provides clues to the two main, if not only, true primary sources, which are writings from Edward Winslow and William Bradford. By reading these texts, deciphering fact from hearsay is possible. This is only possible because we have moved from searching for information to filtering information.

Summary

- Locating information used to be constrained by location and library.

- Previously acquiring information, especially primary source information, was time consuming.

- Information is now abundant and easily assessable.

Implementation

The change from searching to filtering is occurring naturally at a guarded pace. To help students stay ahead of the curve, teachers need to deliberately implement filtering techniques in the classroom. This chapter contains the steps needed to make the transition from searching to filtering. The fundamental steps to help this occur include the following:

- Digital literacy is another form of literacy.
- Advanced search techniques, such as Google and control-f, need to be taught.
- There are simple ways of using the work of others.
- There are five criteria for evaluating websites, especially sites such as Wikipedia, which are user created.

Teaching Digital Literacy as Another Form of Literacy

Assuming that a beginning reader can become literate simply by putting a book in front of him or her is inconceivable. Regardless of how engaging the content of the book or how long the child stares at the pictures, he or she cannot become literate without the help of an adult. Furthermore, if a student is taught how to read using only fictional texts, then it is unlikely that the student would be able to fully comprehend a nonfictional text. The skills and structure are quite different. For nonfiction text, a child needs to understand how to read columns and graphics and how to use headings, glossaries, pronunciation guides, and so on. These are concrete skills that need to be explicitly taught for a beginning reader to be literate as a nonfiction reader. In the 20th century, teaching children the skills needed to read and understand fictional and nonfictional texts was enough. But in the 21st century, teaching only these two sets of skills is ineffective and pedagogically unsound.

In addition to learning the skills to read fictional and nonfictional texts, children also need to be deliberately taught the skills to make them digitally literate. Whether adults prefer it or not, youths are increasingly turning to the Internet for information. According to Olmstead, Mitchell, and Rosenstiel, (2011), "Among 18-to–29-year-olds, the internet became the No. 1 platform of choice for news for the first time in 2010. Nearly two-thirds of that age group, 65%, said they got most of their news from the internet. . . . Among those aged 30 to 49, the web is a clear No. 2, as 48% named it as a main source for news, twice the percentage that rely on newspapers (22%)." Educators cannot assume that children will learn the skills of digital literacy, including searching, evaluating, and understanding digital information, on their own. Turning children loose on the Internet is common yet completely irrational. "Bobby, go on the Internet and look up some information for your report on Florida." This statement contains the assumption, probably fairly, that Bobby understands that he needs to use a search engine; however, a Google search for 'Florida' currently provides 1,620,000,000 websites. Bobby needs to find a way to narrow this search to a manageable number, and this falls squarely on the shoulders of today's educators. Teachers can do this by following three simple steps.

Step 1: Explicit Search Techniques

In the past, when looking for information, students simply crossed their fingers and hoped the local library had a book or two on the topic. With the advent of the Internet and search engines, access to information became much more ubiquitous. The dilemma now is how to turn 1,620,000,000 websites into something manageable. Students need to be intentionally taught how to search effectively.

To begin with, students need to learn how to narrow their searches by using precise language. Instead of searching for 'Florida,' Bobby could refine that search to the 'symbols of Florida' to shrink that to 23,000,000 websites. This is a much smaller quantity, but still totally unmanageable. By breaking down a search of all state symbols to a specific symbol, such as the 'state flower of Florida,' Bobby can bring the list of sites down to just a couple of million. By adding a few additional words, such as 'state flower' to the search phrase 'Florida,' he can reduce the total number of sites dramatically. In this example, the number of sites in Bobby's final search was about 3,000,000, which is 0.2% the size of the original search. And more importantly, nearly all 3,000,000 sites are about the specific topic of the state flower and not about planning vacations, retirement communities, or hurricanes, which would have been included in the original search of 'Florida.'

Students are typically familiar with using the guess-and-check strategy in math class, which should also be used for searching. For those who are unfamiliar, students use the guess-and-check strategy to find an unknown. For example, if $5 \times ? = 65$, what does ? equal. To solve this with guess-and-check strategy, a student would first try something such as 5×10 and check if that equals 65. It doesn't. The answer is too small, so the student tries a new guess. If 5×10 is too small, then perhaps 5×14 would work. Seeing that $5 \times 14 = 70$, which is too big, the student would try a guess in between 10 and 14 until finding that $5 \times 13 = 65$.

How does this relate to searching? Searching involves significant guessing and checking, which isn't intuitive for many students. If Maria is researching U.S. presidents, she might search for 'which parties did the presidents belong to.' This is a fine search that may or may not provide the information she is looking for. If it does, she's done; however, if it doesn't, she needs to guess again. A simple change in the search phrase to 'list of presidents with parties' creates a totally new list of possible websites. Again, if this search provides the information needed, she's done, but if not, Maria needs to guess again. A third search phrase might be 'presidential affiliations.' This provides a third set of sites to choose from. Students need to be explicitly taught to use guess and check until they discover a search phrase that provides a list of websites that answers their questions.

Another search technique that is extremely useful for students, especially young students, is including words such as 'kids,' 'children,' or 'student' in their searches. These keywords significantly reduce the number of sites and provide students with a majority of sites that are geared toward their age group. This can also be done using advanced search features as well, which we will touch on later.

A final simple technique to provide students is the use of quotation marks. We used single quotation marks above intentionally, not to be confused with traditional quotation marks used for searching for specific phrases. Using quotation marks around words in a search requires websites to contain that specific phrase. A search of 'red, white, and blue' provides a list of all sites that contain those words. The order, location, phrasing, etc., are irrelevant. However, searching "red, white, and blue" provides a list of sites that contain only the *exact* phrase *red, white, and blue*. In this case, the search with double quotation marks is about a tenth the size of the first search, and all the sites contain the specific phrase.

Children in the 21st century must know, understand, and use these simple techniques, and the techniques need to be taught explicitly. This can be done in a stand-alone lesson or a simple comment over a student's shoulder. Regardless, students need to have the skill set to sort through the abundance of information found on the Internet.

Advanced Search Techniques

In addition to these simple search techniques, many search engines utilize easy-to-use advanced searches. Google, for example, provides a series of options specifically designed to narrow search results. As the Internet grows and collects obsolete remnants, these simple tools will help students develop the necessary filtering traits.

Quite often research data is somewhat time sensitive. Perhaps a student is researching a current election and does not need any information from previous elections. By using an advanced search, a student will find only sites updated over a given time period, such as the past year. This reduces the number of sites and targets only the specific relevant dates.

A second advanced feature that students benefit from knowing about is searching specific sites and domains. Domains include websites ending in .com, .gov, .edu, .org, etc. As students begin to evaluate the quality of their sources, recognizing domains becomes more important. On the surface, a .gov site is probably more credible than a .biz site. Although searching specific domains does not entirely solve the issues of reliability, it is one important tool to use. Specific sites can also be searched. For example the Smithsonian's primary website can be searched using the advanced search to search only the Smithsonian's URL si.edu. By searching the site si.edu, the only results that will appear will be from a page on the Smithsonian's website. This is particularly useful for searching sites that have known reliable content.

Responsible educators do not put texts in front of students that are beyond their reading levels. Reading a difficult text can be not only ineffective but counterproductive. This is why texts that are too difficult for a child to read are called "frustrational." They are just that—frustrating. Why, then, would children be turned loose on the Internet with complete disregard for reading levels? The majority of the information on the Internet is not written by educators or written for students. The advanced search features of some search engines, such as Google, factor in reading levels. Google allows searchers to have the reading levels displayed next to the website links, or search results can be limited to only a given reading level. Providing students with websites they can actually read and comprehend is pedagogically sound and ethically right.

A final advanced search option, which is critically important when searching for images, is usage rights. Responsible digital citizens avoid plagiarism and infringing on others' intellectual property rights. Although the Internet is more policed than it was a few years ago, it is the modern Wild West for many people. Many students are exposed to bootleg videos, illegally downloaded music, and other illegally obtained materials from peer-to-peer networking. It is so common, students may fail to realize that accessing such material is illegal and morally wrong. As educators increasingly use the Internet in the classroom, they need to make a conscious and intentional effort to help students understand usage rights.

A simple way to teach usage rights is through the use of advanced search options for usage rights. Students can select the level of usage needed. The rights generally range from "free to use" to "free to modify and use commercially." These rights are based on the standards set by Creative Commons, an organization that has created copyright rules and licenses that are suited for the Internet. Many educators are guilty of playing loose and free with usage rights by claiming educational immunity and doing so ill-prepares students for the modern world. The consequences of plagiarism in upper grades, post-secondary settings, and the workplace can be quite catastrophic. Students need to be taught the ins and outs of usage rights in a safe, controlled environment such as a classroom.

Control-f

Even before the information overload of today, students struggled to understand the correct depth of reading on the Internet. As the quantity of information has increased, so has this problem. Students tend to fall into two camps. The first group sees a text with many words and decides it is too overwhelming to even begin reading. Other students see a text with lots of words and think they need to read every last word. Although there are times when a reading needs to be attacked with a fine-tooth comb, where each idea is read word for word, there are other times when a simple skim is needed to find specific information. Students need explicit instruction and structured opportunities to skim texts online and in hard copy. Skimming for information on a computer is infinitely easier than with a hard copy. With two simple keys, control-f on Windows and Ubuntu machines or command-f on Macs, the computer does the skimming for the reader. These keystrokes pop up a search window. Rather than reading and reading looking for specific information, students can simply search for keywords. Although using the computer to do the skimming does not replace the work of an actual human, it is an extremely efficient place to start.

Step 2: Use of the Work of Others

Social bookmarking isn't exactly cutting edge anymore, but its impact continues to be revolutionary. After living in a world where bookmarks were tied to a specific computer, it is truly amazing to save a bookmark on one computer and have it available on another. Additionally, not having to worry about backing up bookmarks is a huge relief. Nothing is more frustrating than saving hundreds or thousands of bookmarks over years only to have them all lost when a computer crashes. Furthermore, having to place a bookmark in a specific folder can be stressful. The struggle of deciding whether this chemistry experiment website should be saved in the science or chemistry or experiment folder is overwhelming. Social bookmarking allows people to use multiple tags rather than folders. That chemistry experiment website can be bookmarked with the tags "science" and "chemistry" and "experiment." Social bookmarking solves all three of these problems.

Although social bookmarking has revolutionized bookmarking, none of the praises previously sung explain why it's called social bookmarking or why it belongs in a section on filtering. The social aspect of social bookmarking is that all bookmarks, unless marked private, are public for the world to see and use. (You can see the Engaging Educators' social bookmarks at groups.diigo.com/group/engaginged.)

Through social bookmarking sites, information can be filtered very easily. First, people tend to tag, or bookmark, only websites that are useful.

By searching the tags, you can see which sites have been bookmarked and by how many people. This can shrink the millions of websites down to just a handful, which can be sorted by popularity. Second, social bookmarking can be used to share bookmarks with colleagues. As colleagues search for resources on a given topic, each of them can add their own bookmarks to a group of agreed-upon tags. Rather than having to sort through millions of websites alone, you can work together, sharing and archiving the load for future use. Third, it is possible to follow individuals who have similar interests. By finding those few individuals who have the same interests, whether personal or academic, and following them, you can have much of the heavy searching and filtering done for you. Finally, groups are already set up but can also be easily created to work communally to find and filter useful websites. Social bookmarking is an incredibly powerful tool, and through the social aspect of it, filtering takes on the previous role of searching. We will give you more on social bookmarking in Chapter 14.

Twitter

Microblogging sites, such as Twitter, may be the fastest-growing form of filtering. Twitter requires all thoughts to be expressed in 140 characters or fewer. Although many people mistakenly think Twitter is only for following celebrities, many great minds use Twitter as well. (We are not saying that celebrities can't have great minds too.) Most microblogging sites, such as Twitter, allow for searching. By simply typing a word or phrase into the search bar, you will see all posts over the past few days that contain that phrase. Additionally, handles, or usernames, that contain that phrase will appear. Furthermore, hashtags, which are loosely agreed-upon tags that are normally affixed to the end of a tweet to provide context, such as #edchat and #urbaned, can be searched and followed too. By following a hashtag, all posts containing that tag by anyone will be flagged for reading. In addition to searching, a simple question asked to a well-crafted personal learning network nearly always provides help in a quest for information.

There is no reason in the 21st century that you need to find all desired information by yourself. By using the works of others, you will find that the impossible job of searching and filtering information becomes more than manageable: it becomes productive and motivating.

Step 3: Web Content Evaluation

After filtering out the useless, irrelevant, and outdated information on the Internet, students must learn to evaluate the Web content. It does not matter how perfectly the information on a website matches what is being searched for if the information is inaccurate, biased, fraudulent, old, inaccessible, or flat-out wrong.

It is all too common to hear educators berating the use of websites such as Wikipedia. The occasional hoax or misinformation has caused many to generalize and think all websites, or at least all user-created websites, are fraudulent. By following the steps below, students can easily evaluate Web content and find sites, such as much of Wikipedia, that are reputable and good to reference. Evaluating websites can be broken down into five general areas of interest.

Purpose: The first area of evaluation is the author's or publisher's purpose. Is the author trying to persuade, inform, entertain, etc.? A good place to look currently, although policies look poised to change in the future, is at the domain name. Is the website a .gov, .edu, .com, etc.? The domains .gov and .edu tend to be more reliable because they come from the government and universities, respectively. Other domains, such as .com or .org, can be just as reliable but require closer scrutiny.

Authority: The second area of evaluation, which goes along with the first and can help illustrate why the agreed-upon areas of evaluation fluctuate from about four to ten, is the authority of the source. As before, is the author a major university, a media network, or a guy working out of his house? Many sites like Wikipedia are the latter, but that does not singlehandedly discredit them. On sites that are less credible on the surface, students must look for resources and references. Most reputable websites, such as Wikipedia, provide a list of references at the bottom of the page.

Objectivity: The third area of evaluation that deals with the author is objectivity. Is the author objective, or does the writing reflect a bias? The bias can be either explicit or implicit. This book is intended to transcend politics and focus on successful 21st-century teaching and learning, but politics is a great lens into objectivity. Rush Limbaugh has an explicit bias to the right, and NPR tries to maintain neutrality but tends to have an implicit bias to the left. A bias is not a deal breaker, but it is imperative that the reader be aware of it and take it into account.

Currency: As the World Wide Web cruises through its twenties, the quantity of leftover Web debris is staggering. Old does not equal irrelevant unless current information is needed. For example, a Nirvana fan page from the early 1990s could be a useful resource for someone researching that group. However, the state song of Colorado has changed since the days of Nirvana. In the early 1990s, the state song of Colorado was "Where the Columbines Grow"; in the mid-1990s, the state added John Denver's "Rocky Mountain High" as a state song. In one case, the old information is very relevant, and in the other case, the old information is obsolete. Perhaps these facts are not overly important, but they illustrate the point. Many websites have the date of the last modification time-stamped on the bottom. It is also possible to use an advanced search through sites such as Google to limit the search results for websites within a given time frame (see Step 1). As a last resort, if the date cannot be confirmed, it is always possible to look for other webpages that corroborate the information.

Accessibility: To put it simply, some websites are easier to navigate, faster to load, and easier on the eyes. When forced to choose among numerous sites of equal relevance, we recommend choosing the sites that are more accessible. As Web 2.0 becomes the mainstream and the Internet becomes easier to publish on, students and teachers need to think about the accessibility of the content they create as well.

What Have We Learned?

- Teach explicit search techniques including advanced searching and control-f.
- Use the work of others through networks such as Twitter and Diigo.
- Evaluate websites by looking at the site's *purpose, authority, objectivity, currency,* and *accessibility.*

What Now?

Where are you with your searching versus filtering? Do you still spend your time searching, or are you spending your time filtering? Below are three steps you can follow to move from merely searching into 21st-century filtering.

NOVICE:
Start by assessing how you search or filter information. Before trying to implement this with others, work on implementing these filtering tools in your own practice.

INTERMEDIATE:
Begin implementing explicit activities to encourage students to use advanced search techniques and searching the works of others. These lessons do not need to be lengthy. Two minutes here and there really add up. Squeeze these tips and tricks into the down time before a transition.

EXPERT:
Be sure students are evaluating Web content on a regular basis. This should begin as explicit instruction. Through repetition, this should become more natural, eventually becoming a subconscious occurrence. Ask yourself if this is happening subconsciously yet, and if your answer is no, keep practicing.

9 Anecdotes

Imagine this scenario for a moment: The year is 1994. You have no Internet access. Your assignment as a high school senior is to write a 10-page position paper. The thesis you have chosen is "The Central Intelligence Agency and its counterespionage efforts have failed to keep the United States safe during the second half of the 20th century." Like any studious twelfth grader, you head to the local library to do some searching for resources. Because the library has just recently converted to a computerized card catalog, the searching goes a little faster. The results, however, are not very positive. There are three books and a couple of magazine articles that *might* help in some way. Unfortunately, the only way to know for sure is to read them. Yes, the books' indices might help you narrow things down a bit. But that is no guarantee. There's a good chance you'll spend a good deal of time wading through this information without your efforts bearing fruit. And if, by some likely chance, the books and magazines don't have enough useful information, you're now presented with a whole new level of nightmarish searching.

We share this true example from Ben's high school days in an attempt to illustrate the changes that have occurred with the coming of the Information Age. Before the advent of the Internet and before "Google" became a verb, many students charged with research projects had to spend vast amounts of time finding the information they needed. Research often turned into a wild goose chase of sorts, as students scrambled frantically to find anything relevant to their work. It could be a time-consuming and frustrating process.

This is no longer the case. Information of all kinds is accessible with just one Web search. However, we have entered a scenario in which the opposite is true—whereas before information could be a challenge to find, now there's an abundance of it. Because of this, the shift from teaching students how to search to teaching them how to filter is critical. The following anecdotes illustrate why and how this should happen.

Filtering for Teachers

Requiring young children to perform research in a timely manner can be challenging, especially when they have not developed the filtering skills necessary to search efficiently and effectively. We have found two ways to speed up the research process when working with younger students: Google Custom Search and Diigo. Of course, we do believe that teaching filtering skills is important, but if there's a research project to be done and time is of the essence, these two tools can help you a great deal.

Google Custom Search

Google Custom Search (www.google.com/cse) allows you to create your own search engine. Whereas a Google search scours the entire Web for results, a Google Custom Search searches only the sites you tell it to. We used it when teaching our students about the 2010 tsunami and the after-effects in Japan. After finding about a dozen sites with useful information, we created a custom search engine that would return results from only those twelve sites. This narrowed the breadth of the search considerably, making research time more efficient and effective. We could trust that the information students were gathering was relevant and meaningful because we had done the filtering ourselves in advance, choosing only sites we knew would be reliable and useful.

Diigo

Another way we've provided filtered information for students is by using the social bookmarking site Diigo (www.diigo.com). In advance of the research project, we used Diigo to bookmark the sites we wanted students to search, making sure to save them all with the exact same tag. In this case, students were learning about the state of Michigan, so we simply tagged each bookmark with "Michigan." From there, we gave students the Web address to these bookmarks: www.diigo.com/user/bcurran/Michigan. We told them that everything they would need for the project could be found within those sites. This required slightly more work to filter and locate valuable information on the students' part than the use of Google Custom Search. They had to do more clicking and exploring to find the facts they needed. This gave them good practice evaluating websites to determine relevance to the project. Students became very efficient at deciding if a site could help them or not based on its title and a quick scan of the page. This practice was effective and did not slow them down because they were looking only at sites we had chosen in advance as opposed to the entire web.

Explicit Searching Skills

Every project we run has a "hook." A hook is similar to the traditional college education school phrase "anticipatory set." The hook is designed to grab students' attention, activate their prior knowledge, and get them excited about the project. However, with this searching activity we hooked students by frustrating them. We had been casually providing help and feedback as students worked on their exhibitions (more on exhibitions in Chapter 12), but we noticed many students still searching in inefficient ways. Google is incredibly powerful, and even with students' poor search techniques, they found their answers most of the time, but we knew with a little help we could minimize their confusion and the time it was taking them.

We based our activity on Google's own searching puzzle called A Google a Day (www.agoogleaday.com). These puzzles involve searching the Internet for answers; however, the puzzles are set up to be multistep questions. You have to solve the first part to understand the second step. The A Google a Day puzzle at this moment is, "In what Broadway musical did the wife of the star of 'Ferris Bueller' have the lead role for one year, beginning in 1979?" First, you have to figure out who the star of "Ferris Bueller" is. Then, search for his wife. Next, using the wife's name, search for which Broadway musicals she has performed in. Finally, figure out which of those musicals she was in in 1979.

On the first day, we provided no instruction whatsoever. We wanted students to struggle so they would be more receptive to our mini-lesson the following day. We provided students with a half sheet of paper with a question and a spot to record their search term history. A question we gave some groups was, "According to the Brooklyn *Daily Eagle*, how much would you have paid to cross the longest suspension bridge in the United States when it first opened?" A typical search phrase for students was, "How much did it cost to cross the brooklyn daily suspension bridge?" As you can imagine, this didn't provide much in the way of useful information. We actually had to cut the activity short because the students were becoming too visibly frustrated. We wanted to create some frustration but not enough to turn them off from the activity.

On the second day, we started with a brief mini-lesson in which we presented some suggestions on how to search. We talked about looking for keywords. We showed them how to use Google Advanced Search and modeled how to locate more complex information through a series of multiple searches. Finally, we showed them how to use control-f or command-f to locate specific words or phrases on a page. Following the mini-lesson, students conducted the same activity as the first day. To say that all their searching and filtering problems were cured would be a lie, but there was significant improvement for many groups. The level of frustration was visibly lower. The biggest success was with control-f and command-f. Students used that skill throughout that day, and we have seen them using it since.

These activities took about an hour of class time. We know that class time is valuable, and this activity did not tie in with math, reading, social studies, etc. However, it does meet numerous CCSS College and Career Readiness Anchor Standards for Reading:

- Read closely to determine what the text says explicitly and to make logical inferences from it; cite specific textual evidence when writing or speaking to support conclusions drawn from the text.

- Interpret words and phrases as they are used in a text, including determining technical, connotative, and figurative meanings, and analyze how specific word choices shape meaning or tone.

- Integrate and evaluate content presented in diverse media and formats, including visually and quantitatively, as well as in words

(National Governors Association Center for Best Practices, Council of Chief State School Officers, 2010, p. 10.)

Even if this activity hadn't met any standards, it was an hour well spent. Providing students with these kinds of skills will help them throughout their personal lives and with nearly every subject in school.

As with nearly all projects, we had students reflect on their learning at the end. Without any specific prompting, almost 64% of the students used the word *frustrated* in their reflection. If six out of ten students are feeling frustrated on a non-graded, low-stakes activity, imagine how they must feel on a truly important activity. The following three comments from our fifth graders summarize why activities such as these are important:

> "I think I learned a lot (more) this time than last time. I was very frustrated last time, but this time I was great."
>
> —Jamela

> "I was very frustrated because I couldn't find out the answer. But today we were not frustrated because Mr. Curran showed us some tips about searching on the web."
>
> —Sierra

> "I was frustrated about how some of the information was wrong on some things we looked up on the Internet. I learned that when you need to find something (on) a page you can press command-f . . . I also know that it is hard to find information and I also think it is a good thing because when we get to college we need to know how to research to find an answer."
>
> —Genise

The Amazing Race

The Amazing Race project is our longest-running annual project. We've run this project about once a year for the past six years. It is based, somewhat loosely, on the CBS reality television show with the same name. Over the years, the project has morphed and grown into what it is today. Even from the beginning, however, searching and filtering has played a key role.

Original Version

This project could work with any subject, but we traditionally run it during social studies. The hook for this project usually involved streaming a few clips of *The Amazing Race* from either cbs.com or YouTube.com. We traditionally look for funny videos, which involve people falling down, becoming hilariously frustrated, or slightly injured. The students were children and, let's be honest, those are the kinds of videos they watch on YouTube at home.

After the hook, students were divided into small teams of two or three, and all the teams were then given the same starting question. A question we've used in the past was, "Walking at a normal pace, how long would it take you to walk across the 14th-longest suspension bridge in the world?" This question directly tied into our social studies curriculum dealing with the state of Michigan because the 14th-longest suspension bridge is the Mackinac Bridge, which bridges Michigan's two peninsulas.

This question had three steps, the first two of which involved searching and filtering. First, students needed to identify the 14th-longest suspension bridge. Then students used that information to search the Internet to find out that the bridge is 26,371 feet long. Once they discovered that, they then had to figure out how long it would take to walk it. Students had access to tape measures and stop watches. In the hall of the school, students marked off a given number of feet and timed how long it took to walk that distance. Using that time and distance and the length of the bridge, they calculated the time it would take to walk the bridge.

Following the correct completion of the first question, they received a second question and so on. To add variety to the activity, we also mixed in other types of Amazing Race clues, which can be found on the Internet with a simple search. This year we were studying U.S. cultural regions, so all clues dealt with different regions of the country. A challenge we like to use is the "detour," which involves choosing between two clues with rhyming names. One of the authors of this book provided a favorite "detour." The teams had to choose between "guac" or "chalk." "Guac," as in *guacamole*, rhymes with chalk in this author's world. Without knowing anything more than these two words, the teams had to choose their clue.

If students chose guac, their clue was, "Find three teachers who like guacamole, and according to the California festival bearing the name of the fruit from which guacamole is made, find the year that this fruit became a cash crop in California." This clue involved the fun task of questioning teachers about guacamole and important social studies concepts, such as cash crops. Students searched for the kind of fruit in guacamole. Then they had to search the California Avocado Festival page for information on cash crops. This search lent itself well to an advance search in which Google locates information on a specific site.

If the students chose "chalk," their clue was, "Locate a piece of chalk in the school [which is easier said than done in the 21st century with traditional and interactive whiteboards], and using that chalk, write the names of five games mentioned in the 2010 documentary about games involving chalk, a Spaldeen, and a city." Street games in large cities, such as New York, are an important part of the culture.

In today's world, information is abundant, and the original version of our Amazing Race project was designed to have students locate relevant, accurate information and then synthesize the information into coherent answers.

New Version

We are still strong supporters of the original version of the Amazing Race project, but we realized that we, the teachers, were doing much of the heavy lifting. In the new version, we rectified that problem.

The new version plays just like the original, but in this version the students write the clues. We provide each team with a list of standards, in student-friendly language, from which they have to generate clues. We use a simple Google Sites page with embedded Google Forms to collect the clues. It takes about 15 minutes for us to pick the standards we want met from this project and about 30 minutes more to set up the Google Sites and Forms. This is just about it for our up front work.

Students then search and filter through information to create their own clues based on the different cultural regions listed in our social studies curriculum. The best clue or clues from each cultural region is selected to be the clue used in the actual race. Therefore, there is a distinct advantage to writing good clues. If a group's clue is used, the group members already know the answer. Students work for about an hour a day for two weeks, searching websites, reading their social studies books, and creating clues. For the last week of the project, students compete in the Amazing Race project as mentioned in the original version. In this new version, most of the learning happens before playing the game. The learning occurs from researching and writing clues. This version is much more open ended and student centered, and it provides an opportunity for students to create rather than consume.

Whether students are playing some version of the Amazing Race or working on searching activities, they need opportunities to refine and improve their searching and filtering skills. The quantity of information and the size of the Internet are only going to continue to grow, while the quality of information is going to stay the same at best. Students need to be taught the skills of digital literacy to succeed in the 21st century.

Shift 4: Standardized Versus Student Centered

An Introduction

Our fourth shift toward a 21st-century teaching and learning environment involves moving from a standardized, one-size-fits-all approach, to one that is more student centered. The steps involved in this are not very complicated, but implementing them does require a completely fresh approach to teaching and learning. This approach may be quite different from the style you were used to when you were in school. The results, however, are well worth the effort. By transforming classrooms to a more student-centered environment, you will engage more students, more often, and in more ways. What frequently happens is that people—parents, teachers, politicians, etc.—become convinced that the way school was for them is the way schools should be now. Just because in your past educational experiences students were treated like clones of one another, doesn't mean that's the way a classroom has to (or should) function.

We'll begin this shift by examining these areas:

- There are problems with the "sage-on-the-stage" model.
- There are dangers of standardized teaching as a response to standardized testing.
- Teachers ignore some of the key concepts they learned in college for various reasons.
- Shifting to a student-centered model provides many benefits.

Then, in Chapters 10 through 12, we will do the following:

- Show you how to create a student-centered classroom
- Provide you with examples of student-centered learning activities

The Sage on the Stage

If you received your education any time within the past 100 years, most of your teachers, especially in secondary school, stood in front of the class and lectured—usually for long periods of time. You most likely were expected to take notes. Everyone was expected to be quiet and listen. Let's examine this model, and the problems with it, in a little more depth.

First, no matter how many students are in the class, if a teacher is lecturing, there is a good chance that a number of students aren't listening and, therefore, not learning. It's completely natural and understandable for a teacher to believe that his or her students are hanging on every word. But of course, that isn't always true. Suppose you're teaching a class of twenty-five students a lesson on the United States Civil War. As a history teacher, you are probably fascinated by this topic and are consumed with providing dates, facts, names, and details to your students. Your expectation is that, as you spend the entire period providing them with notes they should treasure forever, they are focused, writing furiously, engaged, and above all, learning.

We've all done it. And sometimes, a *short* lecture is necessary. We wouldn't propose eliminating the approach altogether. But consider this: when a teacher is lecturing, a percentage of students are probably not listening to a word. Another few of them are probably trying to listen but don't *understand* a word. And others probably stayed up too late or missed breakfast or are fighting with their mothers or boyfriends or—you get the point. Potentially, only a portion of your class—seven students? eight?—is actually listening and learning. Even if the teacher stops every few minutes to ask students questions, he or she is probably calling on only a fraction of the class. This leaves a large number completely ignored.

These are, of course, hypothetical estimates. But they are not entirely unrealistic. Even if only two or three students are neither listening nor learning, that is still far too many to be acceptable. Are you satisfied teaching in a way that leaves a majority—or even just one—of your students scratching their heads, disinterested, and disengaged? Are you comfortable squandering precious minutes and hours of your students' education? Most certainly not. But these things are happening whenever you use large chunks of time talking directly to your students. Whether you teach history, math, science, literature, or elementary school, when you stand in front of an entire class and talk, you're running the risk of losing the attention of a large percentage of them. You're running the risk of wasting their time—and yours. A student-centered approach can alleviate these problems and bring about more meaningful learning experiences.

The Negative Impact of Standardized Testing

Don't let this section's title fool you. This portion of the book is not intended to be a rant against the negative impacts of standardized testing and potential concerns about Common Core State Standards (CCSS). There are, of course, many things to say about these topics, but we are focusing only on this idea: *just because the tests are standardized and the core is "common," your teaching does not have to be either of these things.*

Standardized testing and common standards create a trap for many teachers. Falling into this trap leads them to standardize their teaching, offering up a one-size-fits-all approach to their students. They teach their students as if they were all the same. Day after day. Year after year.

The pressure to perform and to boost students' achievement on these tests, of course, is enormous. We feel it every day in our own classrooms. However, somehow the view of the forest is lost among the trees—teachers forget that their students are anything but "common" in their interests, learning styles, temperaments, personalities, and so many other ways. Unfortunately, though, many schools have become factories that provide the same kind of instruction to every child. Students are treated as a product created on an assembly line, as if producing children who excel at test taking is the equivalent to achieving and learning. And while this may lead to increased test scores, we can't help but wonder: "At what cost?" The world in which we live certainly doesn't need test takers. It needs thinkers, learners, problem solvers, doers, innovators, and creators.

The purpose of this section is to help you avoid this trap. By no means are we recommending that teachers ignore standards, tests, or direct orders from administrators. We will, however, provide a way to create a student-centered environment that is grounded in standards and current best practices. This will allow students to excel on state and national tests *and* develop all the skills they need for success. There are many ways to make this happen. Standardized testing does not require standardized teaching.

Ignoring the Research

Anyone who earned a teaching degree within the past thirty years learned about Howard Gardner while in college. He is the researcher behind the theory of multiple intelligences. In short, this theory posits that everyone learns differently, and the ways can be broken down into categories, including visual, auditory, and kinesthetic (Gardner, 2011). The professor who taught you about Gardner probably stressed that his work was groundbreaking and that teachers must keep the learning styles in mind when designing lessons and activities. If you're like us, that professor taught you how to take a general topic, such as life science, and create learning activities that would appeal to different learning styles.

This is valuable learning, for sure. Gardner's work has tremendous value for educators in the 21st century. However, the problem is that many of us forget all about him when we get into the classroom. (Maybe because that professor was lecturing.)

Why standardize teaching when students learn in so many different ways? We're doing them a disservice by disregarding Gardner's work. The idea of a student-centered classroom, where students have individualized learning plans and opportunities to demonstrate their learning in different ways, is not groundbreaking. It's an idea that's been around for years and that has been put into action in terrific, high-achieving schools across the country. That is yet another reason to transform from standardized teaching to student-centered learning.

The Benefits of Student-Centered Learning

Learning is supposed to be fun, and it's supposed to be something that schools help students learn how to do for the lifetime that awaits them outside of school. Never has this been more important than now. Whereas a standardized approach to teaching and learning produces students who are disengaged and ill prepared for life and work beyond school, a student-centered learning environment creates learners who are:

- self-motivated
- high achieving
- independent
- creative
- empowered
- confident
- engaged
- lifelong learners

Is the standardized approach to education doing the same? We don't think so. Students learn in so many different ways. And they deserve opportunities to demonstrate their creativity and intellectual abilities. They deserve to be the central focus of the educational process. In Chapters 11 and 12, we will explain how to transform your classroom from a standardized environment to one that is completely student centered.

What Did We Learn?

- It is time for the lecture-heavy sage-on-the-stage approach to teaching to be used far less frequently. It leaves a large number of students behind, lost, and disengaged.

- One by-product of standardized testing has been the standardization of teaching practices. This is unnecessary and detrimental to students.

- Howard Gardner's theory of multiple intelligences has tremendous value for teachers and is a key component of a student-centered classroom.

- The benefits of a student-centered approach are numerous.

Implementation

How do you go about transforming a classroom from standardized to student centered? In this chapter, we'll start with an overview that describes the key components of a student-centered classroom. Then we'll tackle the question "How do I make this happen?" We'll share the fundamental steps, which include these:

- Thoughtful designing and planning of standards-based lessons, units, and projects is necessary.
- Setting up classroom routines allows for students and their learning to be the central focus of all you do.
- Less lecturing and more student activity is a must.
- Students need to take control of their own learning by exploring topics and content on their own, particularly topics that they're interested in, rather than topics chosen by the teacher.
- Students' interests should be used to individualize student learning through the use of learning contracts.
- Assessing student learning in an equitable and meaningful manner is important.
- There are simple answers to address the concerns of administrators, parents, and students.

Before we go any further, we'd like to pause and give you a peek inside a student-centered classroom. Many of its components wouldn't be clear just walking through or passing by the room. However, pausing to spend just a short time inside a student-centered environment will reveal that it's unique, fascinating, and exciting.

What Does a Student-Centered Classroom Look Like?

Because this transformation could incorporate some routines and approaches that might be unfamiliar, let's start with an overview of what a student-centered classroom might look like. Of course, just as every student is different, so is every teacher. All these elements might not work for every classroom or every teacher. Figure 11.1 gives us a general overview

Choice: In a student-centered classroom, students have regular opportunities to make choices, including choices about what they learn and how they learn it.

Individualization: Students learn in many different ways. In a student-centered classroom, students are encouraged to learn and to demonstrate what they've learned in ways that best suit their individual learning styles.

Thoughtful and Intentional Planning: A student-centered classroom is not a free-for-all. Teachers in these classrooms work incredibly hard, not just during class but before and after as well. The amount of preparation and planning that takes place is evidenced by the quality of student work and the level of students' engagement. Everything is carefully thought out in advance. Planning is paramount in a student-centered environment.

Student-Driven Conversations: You'll hear a lot of talking in a student-centered classroom—in the form of meaningful conversations—between teacher and students and also among students. You'll hear a lot of questions, and these questions are asked by and of students. The teacher often manages the conversation, but the students and their thoughts, ideas, and questions determine the scope and direction of the conversation.

Exploration and Discovery: Instead of the teacher or textbook giving the answers or information, students discover ideas through inquiry and exploration. They regularly figure out solutions and answers completely on their own.

Evidence of Learning: Tests and quizzes are necessary sometimes, of course. But the centerpiece of assessment in student-centered classrooms is student-created "learning artifacts." Students complete these products to demonstrate in-depth knowledge and understanding of key topics. Producing learning artifacts involves higher-order thinking skills and creating them often requires long periods of time.

A Focus on Student Thinking: Every day in a student-centered classroom, the focus is on the ultimate goal of student thinking. Every activity, lesson, and project is geared toward deepening and strengthening students' critical thinking skills. Students analyze, question, explore, and evaluate on a regular basis. Developing these skills is the central purpose of a student-centered classroom.

Figure 11.1 Features of a Student-Centered Classroom

of a classroom with students at its center. We will provide a more in-depth description of how to bring these elements to life later in the chapter.

Now that we've shared some details about what a student-centered classroom looks like, it's time to explore *how* to put the learning in the hands of students. It all begins at the end. Allow us to explain.

Step 1: Planning a Student-Centered Classroom

As previously mentioned, an incredible amount of planning goes into the management and execution of a student-centered environment. A great deal of this is not obvious to a casual observer. However, any attempt to empower students in the ways we've described *without* careful and intentional advance planning will greatly reduce the benefits.

Obviously, a student-centered classroom should involve choice and freedom to explore topics of interest. However, in public school classrooms this is not always completely possible. As much as we'd like to recommend starting each school day with the question "What do you want to learn about today?" we know that's not realistic.

Teachers are expected to teach standards. And there's nothing wrong with basing teaching on standards—teachers need these standards to guide them. Without standards, many teachers would feel as if they were flying blind. Fortunately, teaching that is rooted in standards is completely compatible with a student-centered approach, and our method of planning for student-centered learning addresses this.

The best way to plan student-centered learning activities is in units. And a great way to plan a unit is through the use of "backward design." In their book *Understanding by Design,* Jay McTighe and Grant Wiggins (2005) lay out this method in detail.

Here's our guide to planning for student-centered learning activities, including a handy form to assist you.

Begin with the End in Mind

The key is to choose the outcomes *first*. What will students be able to do when you're done with your unit? What will they know? How will they demonstrate that they know it? (More on assessment in a bit.) Planning with the "end in mind" will result in clear lessons that are focused on the skills and concepts that you are required to teach. Such planning also allows for a lot of creativity. Once you know all your work will be tied to standards, you're free to create whatever path to that end you'd like. The path we suggest, of course, is a path paved by you, with students leading the way.

Arrange the Scaffolding

Once you know what you want to accomplish at the conclusion of your unit, next decide how much support you will provide your students. Depending upon their age, maturity, and experience working independently, students require varying levels of support.

Students who are younger or have special needs will obviously require more support, as will students who are being asked to work independently for the first time, regardless of age. In the planning stages, deciding how much assistance, or scaffolding, you are going to provide is very important.

For instance, you will need to answer questions such as these:

- Who will be in charge of finding the resources, you or the students?
- Will students complete research using search engines, or will you provide a list of links or design a search engine?
- Will you give mini-lessons to provide content knowledge to students during the unit?
- How much modeling will take place? (e.g., will you model how to search properly or write a proper paragraph?)
- How many choices will students have in terms of working options (individual, group, etc.) and creation options (how they'll present their learning)?

There are more ways to provide support, of course, but it is critical to know in advance how much you are going to provide, and regardless of how much scaffolding is provided, the emphasis must remain on the students. There still should be choices for them to make, time to explore and discover independently, and a focus on individual learning styles.

Prep the Launch

In the planning stages, after spending time thinking about how the project will end and how much support you will provide, there should also be time spent deciding how the unit will begin. Having a great introductory activity, or "hook," at the start of a unit serves several purposes. First, and most important, it creates excitement. In addition, a great hook sets the tone and creates buy in. Finally, it provides the necessary background from which the project can emerge.

Deciding how to launch a unit takes some creativity. One of our favorite launches involved teachers dressing up as characters from a short story. But a launch doesn't have to be anything intricate. A great video, a guest speaker or Skype visitor, a newspaper or magazine article, or a powerful question— all can make for exciting introductory activities. The important thing to remember is to capture students' interest.

Manage Expectations

By implementing a student-centered classroom, you are possibly venturing into new territory. And though the educational journey is certain to be exciting, some routines and expectations need to be laid out in the beginning of your adventure. When planning your student-centered activity or project, communicate to students what you expect of them. The routines and scaffolds you've planned for will need to be explained to students at the beginning, so plan on doing this shortly after the launch. Depending upon students' experience with student-centered learning, you may need to model or role-play certain concepts: how to handle cooperative learning, how to effectively take notes, how to select a resource, etc. Make a plan for all these things so no stone is unturned.

A Note About Time and Rigor

Knowing how long a project or an activity should take can be tricky. In our experience, student-centered work always takes a little longer than we expect. When you're first starting out, it can take *a lot* longer than expected. In the early stages, you're going to have to feel it out for yourself, but setting some checkpoints as you plan can be helpful. Checkpoints are deadlines for

```
Unit Title:

What standard(s) are you teaching?

What will students demonstrate at the end of the unit?

How long will this take?

How will it be launched?

Scaffolding?

How will you assess?

Expectations to model:
```

Figure 11.2 Content Planning Form

smaller parts of the project. For example, the outline might be due on Tuesday and the rough draft on Thursday. Once your students get used to working in this new way, the pace will speed up and these checkpoints will become less necessary. This will happen faster with older students, naturally.

In addition to checkpoints, it is sometimes necessary to put in "firebreaks" to slow some students and keep the class at relatively the same point. This is especially helpful with younger students or students who are used to teacher-centered environments. With the example above, you might establish a firebreak after the outlining step. Explain the outline requirements to students, set them to work, and do not explain the next step beyond the outline until a given day or number of students are ready.

Another thing to keep in mind when you're planning is how rigorous to make your student-centered work. Again, your first attempts should not be too rigorous. Plan to increase the complexity and challenge of your work as you move forward.

Figure 11.2 shows the contents of the planning form we created.

Some Possible Approaches

Several models exist that fit very well with a student-centered approach:

- Project-based learning
- Inquiry-based learning
- Challenge-based learning

Step 2: Rethinking Classroom Routines

Classroom routines need to be revitalized when transforming from a standardized environment to one that is student centered. The first shift that needs to happen is to move the spotlight from the teacher to the students. Lecturing and any activity in which only a few students are actively engaged at any one time need to be reduced or removed. The ultimate goal for a teacher in a student-centered environment is to spend as *little* time talking as possible and for students to spend as *much* time actively learning as possible.

Now that you've taken Step 1 and refocused your planning procedures, here are our recommendations for reorganizing your classroom routines to help create a more student-centered classroom.

Unit Launch

As described in more detail in the previous section, this will involve perhaps an entire hour engaging in exploration so students are hooked and excited. The "hook" is followed by a thorough explanation of the requirements of the unit, making sure all students understand the unit objectives and what they are responsible for doing during the course of the unit.

We always recommend a project guide. This doesn't necessarily have to be a packet of paper; it could be a website or wiki.

Work Sessions

Once the launch is complete, work sessions begin, and this is where the magic starts to happen. Work sessions make up the majority of your time, and they are driven by students. Once you have informed students exactly what they should be working on and what they're expected to do, work sessions begin. This is where the exploration, discovery, and inquiry come in. The number and length of the work sessions depend upon what your unit entails.

The Teacher's Role

The teacher's role during work sessions begins with a mini-lesson. During the mini-lesson, the teacher presents *one* concept in a brief (under five minutes) presentation. The mini-lesson can be planned during the planning phase, or it can be impromptu. An impromptu mini-lesson involves something new that the teacher wants to add to the activity. Another way an impromptu lesson plan can originate is from the teacher's observations during the previous day's work session. Perhaps he or she noticed students were leaving something out of their projects or that a large number of students needed help with something specific. Sometimes a routine will need re-emphasis. These observations become a teaching point that the teacher clarifies during the mini-lesson. Resist the urge to teach more than one topic per mini-lesson. Keep a list of things you need to teach, if necessary, so you'll remember what you need to cover in the future. But hold yourself to only one topic during each mini-lesson.

Following the mini-lesson, the teacher really goes to work. While the students are working (independently or in small groups), the teacher circulates, making contact with as many groups or students as possible. During these *short* (remember this is *their* work time; value it by keeping interruptions to a minimum) conferences, we've had good luck asking the question that author Carl Anderson (2000) recommends asking in his book about teaching writing, "How's it going?" This allows the students to take control of the conference and share successes, concerns, or questions. Again, the teacher should limit the amount of talking he or she does during this conference. If the teacher's answers are needed, that's OK, but it's important that the students control the conversation and ask questions so the students drive the learning, rather than the teacher just giving away the answers and telling the students what or how to do things.

At the end of the work session, the teacher should bring everyone together for a short reflection. It's important that students reflect on a daily basis. Reflection prompts can be short and can vary from day to day: What did you work on today? What did you accomplish? What did you learn? What do you need to do better tomorrow? Having students keep reflection notebooks is a great idea, but our students have enjoyed blogging reflectively. An added benefit of digitizing the reflection is that the reflections can easily be collected into a digital portfolio. (See Chapter 2 for information about digital portfolios.) The end of the work session is also a great time to administer a short exit ticket or formative assessment, if one is needed. These can help inform future mini-lessons, as well.

Some teachers or classes require a little more structure during their work sessions. This can be achieved through daily planning logs (or digital forms). A board or poster of progress can help, too.

The Students' Role During Work Sessions

It may seem obvious that the students' role during work sessions is to work, but there's a little more to it than that. Students have to be well prepared so they know what they're supposed to be working on. The expectations and routines have to be reinforced on a regular basis through mini-lessons. They have to know their role well. Even with older students, you cannot expect them to instantly transform from note takers during lectures to active learners during work sessions. Knowing how to work independently is a skill they will need help with. This is where planning, scaffolding, and teaching mini-lessons come in. Effective planning around how you're going to support students to improve their independent learning skills and how you're going to help them learn these skills is critical.

Students should feel empowered during the work sessions—empowered to explore in whatever way suits them best, empowered to go on tangents if their interests dictate it, and empowered to challenge themselves in ways they aren't used to. Students know you're there to help them (after all, you're constantly circulating!), and they know they can count on you to conference if needed.

"I'm Done"

What do you do when it's three days before the conclusion of scheduled work sessions, and a student utters those two magic words "I'm done"?

We like to borrow from author and literacy consultant Lucy Calkins (2007), who recommends teachers answer with, "When you're done, you've just begun." This serves as a reminder that once students believe they are done, there is still much to do. Whether it's revising, editing, or adding on something, there's always work to be done.

It can certainly be challenging for students to transition into this student-centered approach, especially when they come to find that it's *their* job to do all the heavy lifting—lifting that was previously done for them by the teachers. We've had students get extremely frustrated when we've responded to the question "What should I do next?" with "What do *you* think *you* should do next?" (Young children may be especially vexed, so tread lightly!)

What's most important, however, is for students to know that their role isn't strictly defined. If there's something they want to explore, they can explore it. If they come across something they don't know or recognize, they can try to find it or learn it. No one is going to reprimand them for being "off task" as long as they're working toward the end goal.

That's how problems get solved in the 21st century. That's how innovation happens. There's no one right way to do so many things. School needs to be the place for children to practice this reality.

Demo Days

These consist of a day or two at the end of the unit for students to publicly demonstrate their learning and to learn from their classmates. It's a great idea to invite families and other members of the educational community to Demo Days. We'll talk about this later in the chapter.

Step 3: Empowering Students Through Individualization and Interests

Giving students control of their own learning and giving them opportunities to reflect and grow throughout the course of a school year can have numerous benefits. Even more empowering, though, can be the use of individualized learning plans. A learning plan is a contract between student and teacher. These plans outline specific goals and topics that the student commits to explore.

A learning plan can become a powerful tool in a student-centered classroom. It lays out all the things a student is committed to working on at a given time. A learning plan can be designed to fit the needs of individual teachers and schools, but the key components should remain the same. These include the following:

- Specific goals written in student-friendly language
- An individualized description of how students will meet these goals, including specific activities the students will take part in
- An explicit timeline that lays out what needs to be completed and by what date
- A schedule of meeting times for the teacher and student to check in
- A clear description of the finished product, its content, and its quality expectations

Most important, the plan places responsibility for learning solely in the hands of the student. It serves as a guide so the student always knows what to do, what to be working on, and when it needs to be done. It's a roadmap of sorts. And the teacher becomes the tour guide.

But what about the fact that all students need to learn the same things? We live in a world of common standards, so it may seem that the idea of individualized learning plans is completely far-fetched. That doesn't have to be the case. Here are three ways to individualize students' learning plans:

Think About the "How"

Sure, each student is expected to meet the same common standards, but that doesn't mean students have to learn them in exactly the same way. An individualized learning plan provides opportunities to cater the learning to the needs of each individual student. Have great readers? Their plans will include a lot of text and Web research. Have auditory learners? They'll use podcasts and video to aid their learning. You can match the "how" to any learning style.

Obviously, you don't just go away. You're there to help find resources, steer students in the right direction, and make sure learning is taking place. But students are in the driver's seat, learning in a way that works best for them.

Also, this process may not necessarily work in all subjects, but if you choose one and start there, you'll see how great it can be.

Plan the End Product

Just like with your own planning, when you plan with students, you should consider the end product of their learning. How will they demonstrate what they've learned?

Integrate Interests

This process lends itself to the inclusion of students' interests. Allowing students the time and space to explore topics that most interest them is a powerful way to engage them in meaningful learning. When their interests are at the center of a project, we have seen students become more motivated, more independent, and more likely to exceed expectations.

Step 4: Assessing in a Student-Centered Classroom

Accountability must be built into all student-centered activities. Students need to know in advance that they will be held responsible for the work they do. We recommend providing rubrics at the beginning of projects. These serve as guides for students as they progress. Then, at the conclusion of students' work, these same rubrics can be used as a means of assessment. Just as you begin with the end in mind when you plan, your students begin their work knowing what is expected of the final product.

But how do you create a rubric for a project that, because of the student-centered approach, could end up looking different for every student or group? It comes back to the key elements of understanding that were identified in the planning stages. These are what matter, not what the project looks like or what tools students used to create a final product. So it makes sense that these elements are what the teacher should assess. It is, after all, the teacher who is in charge of the assessment. Even though the work is driven by student interest, the teacher is still behind the wheel.

One way we like to assess student-centered activities is through public presentation. At the conclusion of a project or unit, students present the work they've done. The audience can be just the teacher and fellow students. However, an extra layer of responsibility and motivation can be added by inviting family members, other teachers and administrators, or even key members of the public (such as an investment adviser to a presentation about the economy). In this situation, you have the option of providing audience members with assessment tools, perhaps a shortened version of the rubric you will be using.

The checkpoints we described earlier can serve as assessments, too. Checking in regularly with learners is a great way to know what they're working on and to hold them accountable. These don't have to be anything formal, either. A two-minute conference can serve as a valuable assessment tool during student-centered work.

These checkpoints can also include students assessing one another and themselves. Building self-assessments into your process can make a big difference in the quality and substance of student work. Allowing students to assess one another's progress is also highly motivational.

Keep in mind your ultimate goal: ensuring students obtain the understandings you laid out when planning the project. Assessment in all classrooms, not just those that are student centered, can take many forms. Whether it involves multiple formative assessments along the way, anecdotal note taking, or end-of-unit summative assessments is up to you (and the requirements of your school).

Answering Concerns

Depending upon the nature of your school or district, your path to creating a student-centered classroom may be fraught with obstacles. More than a few questions may arise from parents, administrators, and students alike. However, confidence in the student-centered philosophy and some thinking about the questions critics might ask beforehand will allow you to persuade the nonbelievers.

Here are some of the questions that may come up, along with our advice on how to respond.

How Can Students Possibly Handle This Much Freedom?

They handle it splendidly, thanks very much, as long as teachers do what they do best—teach. Freedom and independence are critical pieces of the student-centered puzzle, but they aren't handed out to students willy-nilly. Freedom is given the right way, with scaffolding and support.

Teachers should help students learn how to be independent learners. They should teach them how to function in a student-centered environment. Switching from a teacher-centered model on Monday to a completely student-centered classroom on Tuesday would be impossible. Students need to be taught the structures, routines, and work habits that are necessary.

The freedom and independence are earned—and learned. And once students are taught effective ways to function on their own, they've got the skills and habits necessary to thrive in this environment and in all kinds of learning and work environments. Yes, that's right, a student-centered classroom prepares learners for the "real world," the world that awaits them after they graduate.

What About Meeting Standards and Passing Tests?

The work done in a student-centered classroom is firmly rooted in the standards. Standards are where all student-centered units begin, as described in our section on planning units. So this type of environment leaves students well-prepared for standardized tests and mastery of Common Core State Standards.

Take, for example, the poetry video project explained in Chapter 3, in which students created digital interpretations of poems by Langston Hughes. This assignment would certainly be categorized as student centered. Students were in complete charge; the teacher was "the guide on the side." Here are the grade-level standards upon which this project was built (National Governors Association Center for Best Practices, Council of Chief State School Officers, 2010):

- Determine the meaning of words and phrases as they are used in a text, including figurative language such as metaphors and similes.

- Determine a theme of a story, drama, or poem from details in the text, including how characters in a story or drama respond to challenges or how the speaker in a poem reflects upon a topic; summarize the text.

- Analyze how visual and multimedia elements contribute to the meaning, tone, or beauty of a text (e.g., graphic novel, multimedia presentation of fiction, folktale, myth, poem).

(p. 14)

- Include multimedia components (e.g., graphics, sound) and visual displays in presentations when appropriate to enhance the development of main ideas or themes

(p. 24)

Obviously, this short activity involves several standards. This is the case for nearly all activities in a student-centered classroom. Following our planning template, you'll be able to make sure all your student-centered work maintains a solid foundation of standards.

What's the Teacher Doing While Students Are Doing All This Work?

This is one of the best parts about a student-centered classroom. It involves a great deal of independent student work time, freeing up teachers to work with students one-on-one and in small groups. This work can be focused on the students' needs, which are rarely the same for everyone, allowing the teacher a great deal of flexibility. Teachers' work with students can be based upon what the students need at that moment. Teachers may also "interrupt" student work with mini-lessons that can be based upon the needs of the entire class.

To those who have yet to be indoctrinated, it may seem as if this situation would allow the teacher to just sit back and relax while the students work feverishly at the task at hand. This could not be further from the case. Teachers in a student-centered environment are in a constant state of motion, moving from student to student and group to group, teaching students how to work their way through problems, asking questions, informally assessing, and coaching them along. Take a look at this sample of a 60-minute work session for a teacher during a poetry project that involved students making a digital movie interpretation of a poem by Langston Hughes:

9:00–9:05 Teach mini-lesson to whole group about imagery in poetry

9:05–9:15 Conference individually with students to check on their progress

9:15–9:20 After noticing that students were choosing background music that didn't match the moods of their poems, interrupt class to teach them how to identify the tone of their poems and find music that matches

9:20–9:30 After noticing that some students are making errors with contractions in their writing, pull a small group to work on this skill

9:30–9:45 Conference individually with students not met with yet

9:45–9:50 Noticing that several students are ready for the next step in the project, bring whole group together to teach next step in the movie-making process

9:50–10:00 Meet with individual students who feel they are done, to help them review finished products

Make no mistake, done properly, student-centered teaching is a lot of work, but it's meaningful work. By no means is there ever a time when the teacher's not doing much work. Quite the contrary.

What About Children in the Early Elementary Grades—Surely They Can't Be Expected to Function Independently?

We would have to disagree with this assertion. Teachers ask children in the early primary grades (K–2) to work independently all the time. Nearly every teacher of these ages runs centers or stations in their ELA and/or math classes, in which students rotate on their own through a series of locations in the room, performing a different task at each one. Young students can certainly work independently with tremendous outcomes.

Again, it comes down to scaffolding. Would we expect a first grader to work independently on a topic of his or her choice for an hour? Absolutely not—but perhaps for 15 to 30 minutes. Young students who are exposed to student-centered environments will develop skills and habits that will allow them to succeed in higher grades.

It's also a terrific age to integrate choice and interest into the curriculum, encouraging them to explore topics of interest and curiosity. Tony Wagner writes in *The Global Achievement Gap* (2010) that the trait many CEOs feel new hires are frequently missing is curiosity. All too often, opportunities for curiosity, wonder, and exploration are neglected in the early grades. Obviously, we think those things should be part of *all* grades, but they fit perfectly into the early elementary years. Allowing young children to explore, create, and think independently can be beneficial to their development.

How Can You Possibly Run an Entire School Day Like This?

We don't necessarily think you can, or should, run an entire school day in the manner we've described. By no means are we arguing for the eradication of lectures from the classroom. There are times when direct instruction is needed. It all depends upon the situation.

The student-centered approach to teaching and learning involves breaking away from a one-size-fits-all approach. This means letting go of the idea that there's one right way to teach. At its core, a student-centered class-room involves teachers teaching in ways that most benefit their students.

What Have We Learned?

- Feature choice, individualization, thoughtful and intentional planning, student discussion and questions, exploration, inquiry, creation of learning artifacts, and a focus on student thinking in your student-centered classroom.
- Begin your student-centered planning with the end in mind.
- Shift classroom routines as necessary.
- Empower students through individualization and incorporation of their interests.
- Use assessment methods that are student centered, too.

What Now?

You're now prepared to move forward and create a more student-centered classroom. We've laid the groundwork; here are three more steps, arranged by experience level, that you can take to put students in the driver's seat.

NOVICE:

Don't feel as if you have to jump headfirst into this shift. Start small. Think about beginning by incorporating choice into your school day. Even small choices can have an impact. For instance, if your schedule allows, let students decide the order of your daily work. Also, look for ways to incorporate choice into your daily class and homework (e.g., "Tonight, complete either A or B"). Giving students options can help them feel empowered.

INTERMEDIATE:

Conduct an in-depth analysis of the time you spend doing certain things while you teach. (You may need to make a video recording!) Look at how much time you spend talking. Is it too much? Could this time be better spent? And look at how many of your students are engaged at any one time. Are any students ignored?

EXPERT:

Look for ways to make your classroom even *more* student centered. Empower students to teach lessons about the things they've been learning. Have them write the lesson plans, teach the mini-lessons, create the classwork or projects. You'll be amazed what you can learn about teaching by letting your students teach!

Anecdotes

Creating a student-centered classroom is not without its challenges. There are, of course, times when the teacher must control the learning. Standards, curriculum, and district restrictions mandate this. Often, there is just no way around it. The purpose of this section has not been to encourage you to subvert the educational system or to risk your job—quite the opposite, in fact. We believe you can meet standards, satisfy district officials, *and* create a student-centered learning environment. The following anecdotes provide simple and effective ways this could happen. This is not to say that your students should run the show and you sit back and relax while they learn (or don't learn). But rather, if you follow the steps presented in the previous chapter, you can indeed empower your students to take control of their own learning.

The world of today demands independence and individuality from its citizens. As Daniel Pink writes in his book *A Whole New Mind*, a shift has taken place in the global workplace. "We are moving from an economy and a society built on the logical, linear, computerlike capabilities of the Information Age to an economy and a society built on the inventive, empathetic, big-picture capabilities of what's rising in its place, The Conceptual Age" (2006, p. 2). According to Pink, in the future it will be the "right-brainers," those who can empathize, tell stories, design, play, and create meaning, who will dominate this age.

This certainly presents a challenge to educators. If this is what the future holds, if it will be these skills that lead to the solution of global problems and the development of the vision and ideas that will improve our economy and society, then how do we develop the skills in students? We obviously believe that this book serves as a guide. Furthermore, we are passionate about the importance of the student-centered classroom in the educational process.

Though the concept of this type of learning environment can seem abstract to the novice (it is certainly less concrete than those we present in earlier chapters), it is a crucial component in 21st-century teaching and learning. Students must be empowered to learn in their own ways, to discover, to formulate new ideas, and to experiment with their thinking. In a student-centered classroom, these are all routine events.

Here are three anecdotes from our own teaching to provide examples of what a student-centered classroom looks like in action. These stories, which represent the tip of an iceberg, will inspire you to do the following: discover what lies below the surface of the iceberg, provide opportunities for students to play the role of teacher, empower students to make their own choices regarding how to demonstrate their learning, and design projects based around student interests.

Students as Teachers

One way we've had a great deal of success in making our classrooms student centered is by placing students into situations in which they become the teachers. In these types of activities, students are informed that *they* are responsible for teaching content to their classmates. Instead of listening to their teachers lecture and taking notes or reading a specific assignment in a book or completing a homework assignment provided by their teacher, the students lead the teaching. They create the means by which other students engage the content, and they are responsible for other students' understanding.

Although this may seem like an incredible burden to place upon students, it turns out to be an incredibly positive challenge and motivating. Students realize early on that if they leave out key elements or fail to be clear, their classmates will miss out on a learning opportunity. This is a point we make at the outset when beginning to work in this manner. In our classrooms, students seize this as an opportunity, rather than shrinking from the challenge or becoming overwhelmed.

What do student-centered activities look like in action? We'll give you an example from a couple of different classes: a science class studying celestial bodies and the solar system and a social studies class learning about early North American explorers. In the first case, students chose from a list of topics about the solar system, ranging from information about the sun and moon to the causes of tides. According to our curriculum, this unit involved a great deal of direct instruction. The teacher's responsibility was to provide facts and background information while students filled out worksheets and took notes in their science journals. The work with explorers dealt with learning about specific European explorers, including their motives and their impact upon Native Americans. In this case, according to the curriculum, students were to read the chapter in their books independently and fill out a graphic organizer.

We decided that the approaches in both cases were insufficient. They would not engage students and would not lead to a deep understanding of the content, so we decided to revise each activity. Students worked in small groups, and each group chose an area of the unit to research. However, instead of simply filling out worksheets, the culminating assignment was to teach the rest of the class what they had learned.

Here's how we did that.

Lay Out the Expectations and Learning Outcomes

We were very clear in what we wanted, explicitly stating what was to be covered, and letting the students know they'd present their lessons to the class. In both cases, students working in small groups were allowed to choose their topic from a list we provided. We explained exactly what needed to be taught and what the students were expected to know at the conclusion of the project. Just as in our traditional teaching role, we worked backwards from outcomes and started our planning by contemplating what we wanted our students to achieve at the end of our project. We provided the newly minted "teachers" the same opportunity to work backwards. Once each group knew what the class needed to learn, they began to design their work around that. In our work, this was as simple as providing each group with a list of questions that the class was expected to answer at the conclusion of their teaching.

Set the Parameters and Timeline

A student-centered classroom is no different from any other classroom, in that projects cannot stretch out interminably. The parameters and a timeline of what has to be done when must be completely spelled out. A method that worked for us in both classes involved creating a timeline that included a final due date for the entire project as well as due dates for the individual steps along the way. For example, the final project might have been due March 15, but their notes were due March 5 and their rough drafts were due March 10. This kept students focused on critical parts of their work and kept them from spending too much time on individual parts or getting pulled in directions that might not be productive or efficient.

Differentiate as Needed

Some student groups will need more guidance than others, especially in your first attempts at this type of work. Do not be afraid to step in to offer guidance or suggestions, but be sure to back out of the way and let students work.

See the Results

When students became the teachers, their work exceeded our expectations. The work they presented not only exhibited a high level of understanding but also engaged their classmates. The groups each opted to take different pathways toward their goals. Some created multimedia presentations that combined video and still images. Others opted for short audio recordings. Another group chose not to use digital tools at all, but instead created an engaging lesson plan that called upon their "students" to construct meaning through inductive reasoning. Each group was unique and effective. The entire class benefited from this approach—not only because the unit assessment showed that they had mastered the required concepts but also because they were empowered to learn about their assigned topic and teach it in whatever manner they chose.

The Power of Product Choice

When students work on activities and projects, who usually determines what the final product will look like? Chances are, it's their teacher. Common projects might include a typed, 500-word, five-paragraph essay (double spaced, of course); a book report that involves filling out a form and coloring in a reproducible from a workbook (or book report alternatives that have a faux-student-centered feel, such as making a movie poster for a book!); or a research report on a topic of the teacher's selection (or, again, in a faux move, a report chosen from a list of topics) that must be a specific length and whose paragraphs must be about specific subtopics. The students are not in charge of their learning in these situations. These represent very clear teacher-centered assignments.

It is obvious why teachers teach this way. They are required to teach certain topics: Native Americans, five-paragraph essays, story elements, etc. There's no way around it. The result is that teachers often mandate final products whose elements are dictated solely by the teachers themselves. And as a result, the experience is far less meaningful, and the conceptual understanding far shallower, for the students involved. Often, as soon as their projects are complete, the students have forgotten all they learned.

In the cases where content is dictated by standards or curriculum, consider making the work more student centered by providing students with the opportunity to choose what their final product will look like. (See Shift 1 of this book, "Consumption Versus Production," for detailed descriptions on how to help students develop a tool kit for creating learning artifacts.) If students are required to learn certain content, and you're required to teach it, give them a choice in how to demonstrate their learning. Although this demonstration doesn't have to be digital, here are a few digital ideas:

- A podcast
- A narrated slideshow with VoiceThread
- A digital movie
- A collaborative wiki
- An animated short
- A blog

Of course this is just a short list of possibilities, and you'll want to create a list of products that fit your individual work. Furthermore, you'll need to lay the foundation for this type of work prior to trying it out. Students will need to know *how* to make podcasts, blogs, and movies before you try this approach. When they do, your project assignment can be given with a "menu" of options. This menu can detail all the ways students can choose to show mastery of the content, *or* it can leave the choice completely up to the students. In the latter case, the students are completely in control, and they must decide what product best fits the assignment and which one will best show their understanding of all that was required of them to learn.

One example of an activity that tapped into students' creative abilities was a language lesson about idioms. Students were tasked with exploring this concept, determining a definition on their own, and then coming up with a way to demonstrate what they learned. They were given the chance to use any tool or method they wanted. Not only were they highly engaged as they created podcasts and movies, but they also demonstrated mastery of this concept on the closing assessment.

Although this situation involved a slightly more restricted choice, social studies students were learning about early Michigan explorers and were required to create an audio recording that explained what they had learned. Additionally, the audio recording needed to teach others about the topic. Students worked in groups, with each group assigned a specific section of the social studies chapter to use as its starting point. A recording was required to demonstrate what the students had learned, in whatever form they chose. Some opted to create mock news broadcasts or interviews. One group even created a game show. Another, after reading several primary source documents, recorded a "diary" of a member of an explorer's team, which provided not only academic content to the listeners, but thoughtful insight of what the experience might have actually felt like. Overall, students were much more engrossed in their work than if they had simply been required to read the chapter themselves and take notes or listen to a lecture.

A third example demonstrating the power of product choice was explained in Chapter 3 of this book in the section called "Alternative Math Assessments." Here's a brief recap of that section: We wanted to provide an alternative assessment for our students at the end of the year. We didn't want to provide only a standard pencil-and-paper test. To begin this project, students brainstormed a list of what math concepts they had learned that school year. They came up with about forty key concepts. They then brainstormed a list of tools in the tool kit—around 20. Next, we had a lottery in which students were chosen at random to pick a concept and a tool. No two students were allowed to pick the same concept and tool combination. The students' task was to create a tutorial on their selected skills for future students to use. They were further motivated by the promise of permanently saving their products on our class blog. The students provided evidence of their learning, and their knowledge of the concepts increased dramatically from creating these tutorials. The only teacher constraint in this project was that their product had to teach a math skill from that school year. Every other choice—from tool, length, specific skill, and so on—was made by the students.

The assortment of material students will choose to create once they are given the opportunity provides another opportunity for them to serve as the teachers to other students. And, in our case, and now yours, because these projects were captured digitally, not only are current students able to learn from them but future students as well.

Where Do You Want to Go Today? Tapping into Students' Interests

What if you asked students this question every morning? What if you allowed them complete choice over what they learned about? We can almost hear you laughing from here. "Impossible," most would say. "There's too much content to cover; I have too many demands on my time. There's no way this could work." Granted, it is true that basing all your teaching around students' interests might not enable you to meet standards and curricular demands. However, there are ways to make your classroom more student centered by incorporating the things that students want to learn about.

We've done this through "interest projects." Two to three times per year, students design projects around questions they are interested in answering: "Who is the greatest running back of all time?" "Which is better, a Lamborghini or a Porsche?" "How do people become professional gymnasts?" Our goal is to challenge students academically around their personal interests, so we work with students and parents to design a plan for the project. The plans include details about what the students will learn about and what the finished products will look like. While the topics are completely up to students, we do require that they approach it from an academic standpoint. Students must find resources, take notes, and create visual aids. Finally, they present their work and what they learned at an "exhibition" at the end of the semester. The majority of the work is done independently at home by the students.

Providing students with the opportunity to explore topics that interest them while tying in academic skills such as research and presentation skills benefits everyone involved. The results are often astounding. When given the chance to learn about a topic of interest, students have exceeded expectations and produced high-quality work. Time and time again, whether students are answering the question "What makes Walter Peyton a hero?" or "How can Lady Gaga be considered a role model?" or "What does it take to be an ice-skating champion?" they have amazed us with the depth and complexity of their work.

Imagine, even as an adult, being given the opportunity to explore a topic of interest and being able to take the topic in any direction you wished. Without limits on your curiosity or restrictions on the appearance of your final product, most likely you'd become engrossed. Our students regularly report that working on their exhibitions has been among their most satisfying and exciting experiences in our classrooms. Their parents are impressed, as well, especially as they see the level of independence rise in their children. In the early stages of the project, parents anticipate that they will need to work closely with students and prod them into getting the work done—actions they've often needed to take during other projects in their children's academic careers. However, it often turns out that they need to do none of these things. If their children have chosen topics they truly find interesting, the students take it upon themselves to start working, to ask to go to the library, and to make sure everything is done on time.

When it finally comes time to present their work to their families and their classmates, the students shine. The exhibition projects on Walter Peyton and Lady Gaga were each about 30 minutes long, and the quality of the information, the visual aids, and the students' presentation skills had the appearance of the work of much older students. In the case of both sets of students, I felt that if I compared either of their presentations to the presentations of 90 percent of our district's high school students, ours would have been superior.

Are you concerned that student-centered interest projects may not have a place in today's standards-driven educational environment? Consider the following Common Core State Standards (National Governors Association Center for Best Practices, Council of Chief State School Officers, 2010), all of which are addressed in these projects:

Reading anchor standards:

- Read closely to determine what the text says explicitly and to make logical inferences from it; cite specific textual evidence when writing or speaking to support conclusions drawn from the text.

- Determine central ideas or themes of a text and analyze their development; summarize the key supporting details and ideas.

- Integrate and evaluate content presented in diverse media and formats, including visually and quantitatively, as well as in words.

- Delineate and evaluate the argument and specific claims in a text, including the validity of the reasoning as well as the relevance and sufficiency of the evidence.

(p. 10)

Writing anchor standards:

- Write arguments to support claims in an analysis of substantive topics or texts, using valid reasoning and relevant and sufficient evidence.
- Produce clear and coherent writing in which the development, organization, and style are appropriate to task, purpose, and audience.
- Conduct short as well as more sustained research projects based on focused questions, demonstrating understanding of the subject under investigation.
- Gather relevant information from multiple print and digital sources, assess the credibility and accuracy of each source, and integrate the information while avoiding plagiarism.
- Draw evidence from literary or informational texts to support analysis, reflection, and research.

(p. 18)

Speaking and Listening anchor standards:

- Integrate and evaluate information presented in diverse media and formats, including visually, quantitatively, and orally.
- Present information, findings, and supporting evidence such that listeners can follow the line of reasoning and the organization, development, and style are appropriate to task, purpose, and audience.
- Make strategic use of digital media and visual displays of data to express information and enhance understanding of presentations.
- Adapt speech to a variety of contexts and communicative tasks, demonstrating command of formal English when indicated or appropriate.

(p. 22)

These examples of putting students in charge of their own learning represent a shift away from situations in which the teacher dictates the way learning takes place in the classroom. It is a shift, though, that certainly needs to happen in order to better prepare children for the world that awaits them. Students as passive receivers of knowledge and information can no longer be the norm. A student-centered classroom provides learners with the opportunities to practice the skills they'll need for future success. This environment also challenges, motivates, and inspires students, providing them with opportunities to infuse their interests and personalities into their work. Every time we have put students at the forefront of their learning experiences, we are amazed at how they respond. Creativity, passion, inquiry, and exploration become the norm and boredom and passivity become things of the past.

Shift 5: Isolated Versus Connected

An Introduction

Perhaps no bigger shift excites us than the move from being isolated to being connected. For years, teachers' learning networks consisted of other teachers in their buildings, former colleagues, and former college classmates. Administrators chose the content and time for professional development. Now, we have moved beyond these constraints as educators and also as students. In this section, we'll discuss the implications of moving from being isolated to being connected.

We'll begin this shift by examining these areas:

- Teachers no longer have to function in isolation
- Students no longer have to depend upon one source—their teacher—for information
- The power of the global audience—students are motivated by the fact that others are reading their work
- Collaboration is vital for both teachers and students in the 21st century

Then, in Chapters 14 and 15, we will do the following:

- Provide you with the steps necessary to connect with other educators
- Help you find a global audience for students
- Demonstrate how we've done it in our own classrooms

Start by thinking of the school copy machine. Like the proverbial water cooler, the copy machine used to be every teacher's personal learning network. A group of teachers gathered around the machine in the morning making copies. Inevitably, conversations occurred and ideas were shared.

This was the group of people from whom you learned and with whom you shared your learning. While they were valuable, they consisted of only a handful of people.

If you are lucky enough to have these priceless colleagues, which many teachers are privileged to have, they don't have to go away in this newly connected world. These people will still be standing at the copier every morning sharing ideas, but the difference is that the whole world is out there, too. There are people right now, all around the world, eager to share the latest and greatest teaching tips with you, and believe it or not, they are dying to hear what your ideas are too. Teachers no longer have to function in isolation. We'll provide you with the steps to move from working in relative isolation to total connectedness using simple, modern tools.

Similarly, students in the past had access to the information provided to them by their teachers. The schools, including the teachers, of the 20th century had a virtual monopoly on the content and how it was provided. The schools decided which textbooks to purchase. The teacher decided how to present the material. The teacher provided the mimeographs. Many students thrived or failed due to whether their unique learning styles matched a teacher's unique teaching style. Today, schools still control how the content is taught, but effective teaching allows for student choice. Teachers and schools no longer have to be the sole providers of information. It is relatively easy for teachers to bring in outside experts, other teachers from around the world, and other online materials to provide a diverse set of learning experiences for students. More important, even if schools aren't doing this, students can still find information and experts on their own very easily. We have told our students countless times, "If you don't understand the homework, look it up on YouTube." A search on YouTube right now of "how to add fractions" provides about 26,200 videos to watch. Are all the videos good? No! Absolutely not. But many of them are wonderful. Students are already sitting around at home watching videos on YouTube; they might as well make that time useful. Even better, students could help by making videos of their own. For more information on that, refer back to Shift 1 of this book, "Consumption Versus Production." The Internet now makes it possible for students to find learning opportunities beyond the limitations of the school, classroom, and teacher.

In addition to students learning from others, they can use 21st-century tools to be motivated and inspired. Most people work harder when an audience is involved. Honestly, who would want to write a paper or complete a project merely for a grade? Producing work that will be viewed only by the teacher and perhaps classmates, graded, and then discarded doesn't provide much incentive to produce high-quality work beyond that of getting a good grade. The idea that someone else, someone who really matters, might care about students' work is truly motivating. You might ask who really matters, and from our experience, the answer is anyone who isn't the teacher. It is quite easy to search out "experts" on any given subject for a project. Invite those experts in to watch the presentation or to review the paper. Experts can also be found halfway around the world. We've had great success using the Twitter hashtag #comments4kids to solicit feedback on student work. We've had people from as far away as Singapore—about as far away from Michigan as you can get—review our students' work. More about this in Chapter 15.

There is an important point of emphasis needed in this introduction that should probably be added to all the introduction chapters in this book: Although much of what we describe sounds like fun, it has moved beyond that to essential. Collaboration for teachers and students is vital to the success of both groups. The 21st century is already more than a decade old, and we are still talking about how it is different from the 20th century. The time is now to make these changes. Teachers and students need to be connected to succeed in a 21st-century global world and economy. Such connections make the life of an educator simpler and more rewarding and provide a more enriching, engaging, and authentic education for students.

Summary

- Teachers' personal learning networks now expand beyond the school workroom.
- Students can, and should, learn from others beyond their classroom teachers.
- Students are motivated by an authentic audience for their work.

14 | **Implementation**

Every so often, a song lyric may get stuck in your head. Even more annoying is when you aren't quite sure what the song is called or what the actual lyrics are. Would you rather ask four or 4,000 people for help in figuring out the song? It's safe to assume that you would find the answer more quickly with 4,000 minds working together to solve a problem like this. Although we don't regularly deal with stuck song lyrics in school, the analogy holds true for questions about education.

The pace of change appears to be increasing over recent time. With a click of a few keys and mouse buttons, people can share their blogs, videos, books, etc., to anyone in the world. It no longer takes months and an army of support to propose an idea that goes global. Being a connected educator helps you stay ahead of the curve and catch up with new ideas that aren't yet familiar. Helping students develop these skills to connect and collaborate is critical too. In this chapter, we will provide you with simple, straightforward baby steps to move educators and students from being isolated to being connected; the steps include the following:

- Setting up and maintaining social bookmarks
- Starting a personal learning network through Twitter
- Adding to a personal learning network through blogs

Step 1: Social Bookmarking

Regardless of your profession or how computer savvy you are, if you use the Internet for any reason, social bookmarking is an absolute necessity. It may be so important that if you don't currently have an account, you should set this book down for a minute and create one. As of now, the preferred site for social bookmarking is www.diigo.com. If you are unfamiliar with the phrase *social bookmarking*, it can be succinctly explained as shared bookmarks that are available from any computer with Internet access. Social bookmarking is step one because it serves as the glue that binds and houses your future connections. There are four key reasons why social bookmarking is so important and why it is the first step in a shift from being isolated to being connected.

1. **Storing bookmarks in the cloud:** Almost as annoying as that song stuck in your head is when you've bookmarked the perfect site on a different computer. Many people today use numerous computers throughout the day. In any given day, you might use a work computer, a personal laptop, a family member's laptop, a personal desktop, a friend's computer, a tablet, or a smartphone. If you are still using the bookmarking feature associated with your Web browser, you could have bookmarks strewn across numerous computers. With social bookmarking, your bookmarks are saved in the cloud, which means they are accessible from any device with Internet access. You simply have to type in the correct Web address. For example, we have pooled our important bookmarks at groups.diigo.com/group/ engaginged. Any time we need to access our bookmarks, from any computer, anywhere in the world, we can do so by visiting that Web address.

2. **Using tags, not folders:** Imagine it's Christmas morning, Independence Day, or any other day when your family takes a lot of pictures. You take a picture that has all your children in it and transfer the picture to your computer to file away. Here is where the dilemma starts. Do you create a folder for Christmas of that year? Do you put the picture in a folder called Children? Do you put that picture in a folder that holds all of the photographs for that winter? Do you use a folder for all holidays? If you are using folders, you have a tough decision. If you are using tags, the answer to all of those questions is yes. You apply any and all tags you think are appropriate for the picture, so you might tag that picture Christmas, Christmas 2012, Children, Holidays, Winter 2012. Now that picture is in all those folders or can be searched for by looking for any of those tags.

Social bookmarking allows you to do this with bookmarks instead of pictures. Think about something you might bookmark, perhaps a website that has great resources for teaching the U.S. Constitution. Instead of trying to figure out which folder to save the bookmark into and then remember months or years later which folder you decided on, you can tag that site with any and all useful tags. You might tag it Constitution, Civics, Revolutionary War, Government, 2nd_Hour, and so forth. Tagging makes life easier.

3. **Sharing:** Tagging makes your bookmark collection more usable not only for you but for anyone else who might have the same interests. Social bookmarks are just that, social. Anyone can see and use what you bookmark, unless you mark something as private. Just as others can look at your bookmarks, you can look at others'. Other people might be complete strangers or your colleagues. It is very simple to set up groups so multiple people can contribute bookmarks. Although your bookmarks are there for the world to see and use, they may not be changed or edited in any way. Think about all the people you work with who have similar responsibilities, such as teaching middle school math. What if all middle school math teachers added their bookmarks to a group? The number of useful resources would be incredible. No longer would each of you have to spend time looking for useful sites and resources. No longer would multiple people have to "discover" the same page. Using social bookmarks and thoughtful tags prevents people from having to reinvent the wheel over and over again.

4. **Searching:** As we discussed in Chapter 8 of this book, the Internet is full of useless, poorly made, irrelevant websites. Social bookmarking allows us to see what sites other people have found useful and worth bookmarking. The more people who find it useful, the more people will have bookmarked it. It is also possible to see what other tags have been applied to that site as well. There is nothing much more connected than searching and sharing bookmarks.

As you move into Step 2, we strongly recommend having a social bookmark account already set up. You are going to need someplace to warehouse all the useful information you uncover as you move from being isolated to being connected. More on social bookmarking in Chapter 8.

The Trouble with Twitter

Getting set up and started with Twitter is the easy part. Sticking with it and using it regularly is something many educators have trouble doing. Twitter is incredibly exciting at first, and educators marvel at its possibilities in their early stages of use. However, as time passes, their interest wanes, and we find that they check twitter with less and less regularity.

It isn't easy, but developing the use of Twitter as a regular routine is critical. Once you've established Twitter as one of your professional habits, you'll be hooked. But how, exactly, can you make that happen? Make a commitment to check Twitter on a regular basis. Find a 10- to 15-minute time period that works for you, and spend that time scrolling through your Twitter stream, tweeting, replying, bookmarking, and retweeting. Perhaps this is in the morning while you sip coffee. Maybe a better time is at your desk after school. Regardless, once you make the time and commit to sticking with it, you'll find you're hooked. As one after the other of great resources scrolls across your screen, the power of connecting with Twitter will be displayed, and what once had to be intentionally developed as a habit becomes a regular part of life that you turn to much more often than 30 minutes per week to feed your desire to connect with other educators and improve your own practice.

Step 3: Blogs

Reading blogs was our first entry into becoming connected ourselves. Although the word *blog* is quite mainstream today, many people are unsure of what the word truly means. *Blog* is short for *weblog* and is a website that contains discrete entries in chronological order, with the newest post at the top of the page. Blogs, and many other frequently updated sites today, use RSS, which stands for either Rich Site Summary or Really Simple Syndication, depending on whom you ask. RSS icons can usually be located in the address bar and sometimes throughout a webpage. Quite often they are orange or blue squares with three white arced lines. By clicking on the RSS logo or someplace that says "Subscribe," you can have that blog or webpage sent directly to your RSS reader.

Popular RSS readers include Netvibes and Feedly, both of which aggregate all entries posted to sites you follow. No longer do you have to go and visit each site. Now you simply visit your reader, and all the articles you would like to read are housed in one location. You are able to sort, filter, and star useful blog posts. You can also bookmark them with your social bookmarking account. A great way to find blogs worth following is a tweet asking for suggestions. Using an RSS reader allows you to stay organized and up-to-date in a quick and timely manner. Five or ten minutes a day is enough to keep you current.

Up to this point, becoming connected was not a large time commitment. This next endeavor has the capability of stealing lots of your time; you have to remember that you are in charge. Now that you are reading blogs, it is time for you to return the service. Start a blog of your own. There are several sites you can use, but we prefer Blogger, which is part of Google. Most people who are gently pushed into blogging have the same two fears. The first fear is that you won't have anything to write about. As you use Twitter, read blogs, and have your own experiences, you will have plenty to write about. Depending on how you choose to write, it can almost be thought of as a journal full of reflections on your interests. You can also have a more narrow focus, such as providing resources for others to use. Most important, write about what you care about and are knowledgeable of. Once you start writing, more than likely you'll have plenty to say. The second fear is that no one will read what you write. You'd be surprised. Your list of readers will start out small—probably a couple of friends or colleagues. As you write, and post links to your blog entries on Twitter, your list of readers will grow. Be sure to send us a tweet; we'd love to see what you are doing. People will begin to leave you comments, and blogging will become increasingly more rewarding. Give it a try. Nothing ventured, nothing gained.

Connecting Your Classroom

Making connections with other educators provides countless hours of professional development. This is bound to inspire and improve your practice. However, the 21st century also offers the opportunity for students to become connected. One way this can happen is through global collaborative projects (see more details in Shift 2, "Localized Versus Global"). It can also occur through the use of blogs and Twitter.

A classroom or school blog is a terrific way to share your students' or your school's work with the world. It can offer a window into what's happening, informing both parents and the general public about the amazing learning that is taking place within the classroom walls. Similarly, a classroom or school Twitter account enables short discussions between schools and the aforementioned sharing of student work.

As a connected educator, a whole new world will be revealed to you: a world of accessible and useful professional development, a world where your questions can be answered by educators across the globe after a simple tweet, a world where relevant information is delivered directly to you. Once you've completed this shift, you won't remember what life was like living in isolation.

What Have We Learned?

- Social bookmarking is an invaluable tool for staying organized and gaining new knowledge.
- Twitter is a great place to find and share information.
- Blogs, both reading them and writing them, are a great digital tool for making connections.

What Now?

You're ready to take that next step from being isolated to being connected. You're ready to move from beyond the people crowded around the copier to a personal learning network that stretches around the globe. You're ready to increase your support group from four to 4,000. Depending on where you are starting, here is the next step for you.

NOVICE:
Start by being a consumer of information. Set up a social bookmarking account, such as Diigo. Start following people on Twitter, and find a few

blogs you like to read. If your list of blogs gets bigger than just a few, set up an RSS reader. Be sure to bookmark all the valuable resources you discover.

INTERMEDIATE:
You've now been consuming lots of good information. You have ideas of your own. It's time to start sharing them. Rather than just reading tweets, start sending out your own. Create a blog. It will be rewarding for you and helpful to others. Tweet about your blog, and blog about tweets you read. If you write, you'll get readers.

EXPERT:
You're connected now as an educator. The final step is to provide students with an opportunity to become connected as well. Start a class Twitter account. Have your students blog about school, books, what they've learned in math. Just get them writing. Finally, start thinking about those project ideas you had back in Shift 1 of this book, "Consumption Versus Production." Would any of them be better with collaboration? Help your students develop their collaborative digital tool kit.

# **Anecdotes**

It is easy to feel that working in isolation is beneficial. It can lead to a feeling of independence and a belief that, on your own, you can conquer any challenge that comes your way. This may very well be the case. However, our philosophy is that we are better together. Working as a connected educator, one who works with and learns from others in the field, will improve your practice.

Our anecdotes will provide some insight into the power of establishing a network of educators you can share with and learn from. There is a reason why countless educators call their personal learning networks the best professional development they have ever had. These stories will illustrate that.

 ## **The Power of Community**

In Chapter 14, we walked you through getting set up on Twitter. Now we'll share a way to find invaluable information and resources and to establish yourself as part of the connected educator community: Twitter chats.

A Twitter chat is a regularly scheduled event, organized around a given topic. Usually, these chats are hosted by a moderator, with the week's topic determined and announced in advance. The number of Twitter chats for educators has rapidly increased in the past few years. For many, they are events that can't be missed, conversations so valuable that they become part of educators' regular schedules. Once you get the hang of them, you'll find these chats to be incredibly exciting and fulfilling. This has been the case for us. We join them as often as we can.

All Twitter chats have their own hashtag, a general label preceded by a pound sign (#). The largest and most popular Twitter chat for educators, #edchat, is held twice per week. There are also chats for specific academic subjects (#mathchat, #sschat, #engchat) and specific grades (#4thchat, #5thchat, and #mschat for middle school educators). Educators in several states have organized regular chats. #MichEd, #edchatri, and #njed bring together connected educators in Michigan, Rhode Island, and New Jersey, respectively. As the number of educators using Twitter to connect increases, so does the number of chats.

Taking part in a regular dialogue with like-minded educators from around the world has an impact that can be a bit challenging to describe. As we participate in more and more of them, it becomes clear that teachers are clamoring to discuss and learn from one another. The type of dialogue that is present in chats doesn't often take place within actual school buildings; there just isn't enough time in the day to make that happen. Chats give you a voice, and they give you the feedback you crave. They feed your teaching soul and push your thinking.

One of our most professionally satisfying ventures was starting a regular chat for urban educators (using the hashtag #urbaned). We noticed that though numerous teachers working in cities used Twitter, there was no chat specifically for them. So after engaging in other chats on a regular basis, we started #urbaned chat. This monthly chat brings together educators working in urban areas to discuss relevant topics, such as literacy, poverty, race, and more. Often, the topics we choose are fairly general, such as student engagement or technology. They are approached from an angle unique to urban educators, though, making the discussions much more relevant to the participants.

If you find Twitter chats useful, and you notice the absence of a chat that would be helpful and relevant to you, start one of your own! All it takes is a hashtag (search it before getting started to make sure it isn't already being used), a regular meeting time, and some publicity. Tweet about it regularly leading up to the event, and ask them to tweet it as well. If it's a topic you are interested in, you can be fairly certain that other Twitter users would want to discuss it, too.

Learning from One Another

Although starting a chat can be an exciting and valuable venture, you may find that you do not have the time to commit to organizing and moderating a weekly or monthly chat. You can still make an impact and bring educators together around a common topic by creating a hashtag. We did this as a way to help teachers share resources and discuss issues regarding the Common Core State Standards. We called it #CCchat and it has grown to become widely used, with hundreds of links and resources being shared each week. Unlike a regularly scheduled chat, #CCchat is an all-day, every-day exchange of CCSS-related information. Educators from all over the country have joined in, with many of them sharing multiple resources each day.

The CCSS are not completely understood as well as they need to be by teachers and administrators. Some states are very well positioned to make the transition; others lag behind. CCSS professional development is expensive and often designed to sell a product or a curricular approach. Most educators don't have time to complete a close reading of every official CCSS document; they need help understanding what they really mean. That is where #CCchat comes in. It offers educators a chance to direct their own learning about the CCSS. They don't have to wait for their districts to offer workshops or training. Instead, they take control of their own learning, without having to dedicate a large amount of time to research and exploration. A Twitter search for #CCchat will bring insightful and useful information that educators can use to draw their own conclusions about the CCSS and that they can share with colleagues.

Many educational hashtags offer the same benefits as #CCchat. And because hashtags are completely user generated, anyone can make a hashtag for any reason. If you're a regular Twitter user, and you feel there is a hashtag that would help you in your professional learning, you should create it, publicize it, and use it regularly. Your colleagues and your network will appreciate it. And it won't take long for you to benefit from the community of dedicated educators who use Twitter regularly.

Our First Connections

Our shift toward becoming connected educators occurred without our even realizing it, and it happened in a one-sided manner. We were looking for resources and information that would help us improve our teaching. Up until that point, we were working in relative isolation. Our personal learning network consisted of a small number of teachers, mostly the handful who taught the same grades we did. Social media had yet to make an impact upon our work as educators. In fact, at this point in time, social media had yet to make an impact upon the education world in general. Blogs about teaching were few in number. Twitter was in its infancy and still a few years away from catching on with educators.

Through our graduate school coursework, though, we were becoming aware of technology's looming impact. We stumbled upon a few blogs that were authored by teachers in which they shared educational technology resources and tips on technology integration. These included *Larry Ferlazzo's Websites of the Day* (larryferlazzo.edublogs.com); *Free Technology for Teachers*, by Richard Byrne (freetech4teachers.com); and the *Cool Cat Teacher Blog*, by Vicki Davis (coolcatteacher.blogspot.com). We were also introduced to RSS, a feature of blogs that allows their content to be delivered to the reader automatically with the simple click of a mouse. Using RSS, we subscribed to these first few blogs and immediately became hooked on reading about education and educational technology.

This initial handful of blog subscriptions helped us learn about transforming a classroom into a 21st-century learning environment. From them we received project ideas and exposure to new resources. These first few connections with teachers who were writing about the work in their own classrooms became invaluable to us and helped to both shape our thinking and inspire us to take the leap and shift our teaching. We were now plugged in to the growing community of blogging contemporary educators, professionals whose goals and philosophies matched our own and who have come to be known collectively as "edubloggers."

Over time, as the number of education-related blogs rapidly increased, our small collection of blog subscriptions grew. We now subscribe to more than one hundred blogs, ranging in topic from educational technology to educational leadership to curriculum to literacy and to the CCSS. These connections enable us to learn from educators and agencies located around the world. We are definitely hooked on learning from this network of bloggers, and every chance we get, we help teachers set up subscriptions of their own so that they, too, can connect to the vast quantities of inspiration that await them in the edublogosphere.

The Power of Reflection

Using Twitter and reading blogs are not the only means of becoming connected. A growing number of educators are forging connections as authors in the educational blogging community. These edubloggers add their voices to the conversation by writing posts about their own teaching, about educational resources, about education policy and reform, and much more. These contributions not only provide teachers with ideas and inspiration but also serve as thought-provoking contributions to the educational conversation.

As we have mentioned, reading and commenting on blogs is one way to connect with these educators. However, stronger and more meaningful connections are formed when you join the conversation as a blogger yourself. This can be an intimidating leap for people to make. When we talk to teachers about it, a common response is that they "don't have anything to say." Another is that "no one would read what I write." Both are far from true. The more educators who join the conversation, the better the conversation will be.

We started our blog, the Engaging Educators blog (www.engaging-educators.com/blog/), in March of 2011. After more than 400 posts, our blog rates as one of our proudest accomplishments. Like many bloggers, we went through several phases before finally finding our voice and settling on a format we were comfortable with. Inspired by the many resource-sharing blogs for teachers, we started our blog as a way for us to share tools and links with our readers. Over time, we came to realize that we could make a bigger impact in different ways. Plenty of edubloggers were already sharing these sorts of things on their blogs, so we shifted more toward sharing stories from our own classrooms, commenting on the status of education in the United States, and helping teachers understand the CCSS. In this way, we found a unique place in the edublogosphere, and our blog became a platform for sharing our own points of view, rather than sharing items that readers could find elsewhere.

Once we began blogging, we discovered we *did* have a lot to say and, *yes*, people were interested in reading what we wrote. You will find the same to be true. Whether you blog about your personal philosophy on homework, standardized testing, or teacher evaluation, offer responses to posts that other bloggers write, or simply reflect upon your weekly school experiences, you, too, will find your voice and make connections with readers. Just find a starting point and start writing. Every time you write a blog post, tweet about it. Encourage readers to comment. Make your voice heard. You will discover the experience to be as valuable as we have.

A Helping Hand

Once we developed our network on Twitter, we were amazed by one thing above all others: people's willingness to help. On countless occasions, we have posted questions and requests for advice and assistance and received responses almost immediately. In fact, anytime we have a question we have trouble answering ourselves, we tweet it. And we rarely have to wait long for a reply.

The questions we've asked vary greatly: "Which YouTube editor is easiest to use?" "What's your favorite project-based learning resource?" "Anyone else having trouble logging into VoiceThread?" With a network of colleagues at the ready, you're able to receive valuable information and feedback almost as fast as you click "send Tweet." These responses are much more useful than a simple Google search for the same question, making your Twitter network the ultimate search engine.

One of our favorite instances of receiving help from our Twitter network came when we were preparing for a presentation to elementary school principals about the power of creating a personal learning network and the importance of becoming a 21st-century connected educator. We could have waxed poetically ourselves about all they could possibly learn by using Twitter and social media. However, we thought that testimonials from actual principals and administrators would improve our case. So we sent a tweet with the hashtag #cpchat (Connected Principals Chat) that asked, "Can you please help us out? In one tweet or less, describe the power of connecting with social media?" We were soon flooded with responses from administrators and classroom teachers whom we'd been following with great respect for quite some time—true rock stars in their field. Here's what they said:

- Lyn Hilt (@l_hilt) wrote: "As an admin, Twitter helps me connect w/ forward-thinking, inspiring leaders. Writing and reading blogs facilitates reflection."

- George Couros (@gcouros) responded: "Twitter opens up some amazing connections to others; blogging helps us connect to ourselves."

- John C. Carver (@johnccarver) said: "Best PD [professional development] I have ever been a part of! Time for NEW THINKING!"

- Steve Goldberg (@steveg_TLC) replied: "I learn so much from the smart & innovative people I follow; I often learn from my PLN [personal learning network] who they follow, and that expands my PLN."

- Eric Juli (@ericjuli) wrote: "Ps [principals] should use twitter 4 learning and connecting. Blog 2 be transparent & make vision public."

- Pam Moran (@pammoran) wanted to contribute more than a tweet's worth, so she emailed: "I believe that twitter and other learning social media connect, invite, and inform ideas that principals must explore to lead within today's educational communities. Accessing social learning media advantages principals who choose to share resources, consult, and engage peer to peer with educators from diverse backgrounds—I don't think that an administrator can be at the top of his or her game and not utilize social networks online as a learning tool."

These responses certainly articulated our own opinions, and they contributed greatly to our presentation. They also serve as a tremendous example of how helpful and dedicated the community of connected educators is.

We, the authors of this book, each have earned master's degrees in education (Ben: instructional technology, and Neil: educational technology), have taught for roughly a combined twenty years, are each married to teachers, and have teachers throughout our families. We talk about education with each other, our wives, and our families. Additionally, we work with terrific colleagues who are dedicated to furthering education. We regularly discuss education around the lunch table at work. The point here is, however, that we live as connected educational lives as nearly possible, yet, without expanding our personal learning network beyond our immediate surroundings, we still are teaching in near total isolation. Chapters 13 and 14 of this shift explain why and how to become connected, and the anecdotes shared in this chapter provide a glimpse at the importance of our global personal learning network to us as teachers, educators, and citizens of this planet.

Conclusion

There was a time when the shifts toward 21st-century teaching and learning were optional. They were made by only the most tech-savvy of teachers, those among us willing to take risks, learn new practices, and then execute them in our classrooms. Other teachers considered these techniques cute and, in some cases, gimmicky. Some even developed the misconception that 21st-century teaching and learning was only about the technology. Administrators often took this point of view as they scrambled to keep up by haphazardly investing in interactive whiteboards, tablet computers, and handheld devices. And still, change was seen as an option. This is no longer the case. We cannot afford to wait any longer to make these shifts. The 21st century is nearly two decades old and too many educators and education policy makers still fail to see the necessity of change. They remain wedded to 19th- and 20th-century methods, methods that are simply no longer effective. It is time to understand that 21st-century teaching and learning methods are not optional anymore. It is critical and necessary that these shifts occur. In a changing world, our educational system must change, too. It is this belief that inspired us to write this book. Allow us to review our core beliefs:

It is time to shift our learners from consumers of knowledge to producers of content. The tools for them to make this shift are now readily available and inexpensive. Students will enter a world where it is no longer an option to sit back passively while information is delivered to them. Instead, children need to synthesize information in order to produce learning artifacts.

It is time to shift from localized to global learning environments. We should empower our students to connect with others from around the world, and we should teach students how to effectively collaborate with their global peers.

It is time to shift from teaching students how to search for information to teaching them how to filter information efficiently and effectively. The days of card catalogs have passed. Finding information is no longer the challenge. The challenge now is filtering out accurate, relevant information from the rest.

It is time to shift our classrooms from standardized to student-centered environments. No two students are the same. We, therefore, cannot teach them all the same way and expect to see all students learn.

It is time to shift ourselves from isolated educators to educators who are connected to a broad network of professionals. Your friends at the copier will still be there, but it is time to expand your personal learning network beyond the confines of your environment. Four thousand brains looking for ideas and solutions are more powerful than four.

These shifts are occurring outside of school for 21st-century children. It is time for teachers and schools to join this century. Now is the time; embrace these shifts and empower yourself and your students.

Again, you can interact with the authors and find ongoing content for this book at https://www.facebook.com/EngagedConnectedEmpowered.

References

Anderson, C. (2000). *How's it going?* Portsmouth, NH: Heinemann.

Calkins, L. (2007). *Units of study for teaching writing, grades 3–5.* Portsmouth, NH: Heinemann.

Davis, V. A., & Lindsay, J. (2012). *Flattening classrooms, engaging minds: Move to global collaboration one step at a time.* New York, NY: Pearson.

Friedman, T. (2007). *The world is flat 3.0: A brief history of the 21st century.* New York, NY: Macmillan.

Gardner, H. (2011). *Frames of mind.* New York, NY: Basic Books.

McTighe, J., & Wiggins, G. (2005). *Understanding by design.* Alexandria, VA: ASCD.

National Governors Association Center for Best Practices, Council of Chief State School Officers. (2010). *Common Core State Standards.* Washington, DC: National Governors Association Center for Best Practices, Council of Chief State School Officers. Retrieved from http://www.corestandards.org/assets/CCSSI_ELA%20 Standards.pdf

Olmstead, K., Mitchell, A., & Rosenstiel, T. (2011). *Online: Key questions facing digital news* (Annual report on the state of the media). Retrieved from the Pew Research Center's Project for Excellence in Journalism website: http://stateofthemedia.org/2011/online-essay/

Oxfam. (1997). *Education for global citizenship: A guide for schools.* Oxford, UK: Oxfam. Retrieved from http://www.oxfam.org.uk/~/media/Files/Education/Global%20Citizenship/education_for_global_citizenship_a_guide_for_schools.ashx

Pink, D. H. *Drive: The summaries.* Retrieved from http://www.danpink.com/drive-the-summaries

Pink, D. H. (2006). *A whole new mind: Why right-brainers will rule the future.* New York, NY: Penguin.

Pink, D. H. (2011). *Drive: The surprising truth about what motivates us.* New York, NY: Penguin Group.

Snyder, R. (2011, April 27). *A special message from Governor Rick Snyder: Education reform.* Retrieved from http://michigan.gov/documents/snyder/SpecialMessageonEducationReform_351586_7.pdf

Wagner, T. (2010). *The global achievement gap: Why even our best schools don't teach the new survival skills our students need—and what we can do about it.* New York, NY: Basic Books.

Wujec, T. (2010, April). *Build a tower, build a team* [TED Talks]. Retrieved from http://www.ted.com/talks/tom_wujec_build_a_tower.html